SPURGEON ON THE PRIORITY OF PRAYER

SPURGEON ON THE PRIORITY OF PRAYER

Spurgeon Speaks, Vol. 1

Compiled by
Jason K. Allen

MOODY PUBLISHERS
CHICAGO

© 2021 by
JASON K. ALLEN

All rights reserved. No part of this book may be reproduced in any form without permission in writing from the publisher, except in the case of brief quotations embodied in critical articles or reviews.

These sermons of Charles H. Spurgeon were originally published in the *Metropolitan Tabernacle Pulpit* and the *New Park Street Pulpit*. The compiler has sometimes shortened portions of these sermons and updated certain words and spelling for clarity and context. Scripture references have been updated to the New King James Version.

All Scripture quotations, unless otherwise indicated, are taken from the New King James Version. Copyright © 1982 by Thomas Nelson. Used by permission. All rights reserved.

Scripture quotations marked KJV are taken from the King James Version.

Edited by Kevin Mungons
Interior Design: Brandi Davis
Cover Design: Gabriel Reyes-Ordeix
Cover illustration of Charles Spurgeon copyright © 2015 by denisk0/iStock (484302822). All rights reserved.

Library of Congress Cataloging-in-Publication Data

Names: Spurgeon, C. H. (Charles Haddon), 1834-1892. | Allen, Jason K., compiler.
Title: Spurgeon on the priority of prayer / compiled by Jason K. Allen.
Other titles: Sermons. Selections
Description: Chicago : Moody Publishers, 2021. | Series: Spurgeon speaks ; vol. 1 | Summary: "Volume 1 of the Spurgeon Speaks series collects Spurgeon's reflections on prayer. Known as a mighty man of prayer, his insights will deepen your prayer life too. Presented in lovely editions that you'll be proud to own, the series offers readings on topics of importance to the Prince of Preachers"-- Provided by publisher.
Identifiers: LCCN 2021007459 (print) | LCCN 2021007460 (ebook) | ISBN 9780802426284 (paperback) | ISBN 9780802499578 (ebook)
Subjects: LCSH: Prayer--Christianity--Sermons.
Classification: LCC BV213 .S68 2021 (print) | LCC BV213 (ebook) | DDC 248.3/2--dc23
LC record available at https://lccn.loc.gov/2021007459
LC ebook record available at https://lccn.loc.gov/2021007460

Originally delivered by fleets of horse-drawn wagons, the affordable paperbacks from D. L. Moody's publishing house resourced the church and served everyday people. Now, after more than 125 years of publishing and ministry, Moody Publishers' mission remains the same—even if our delivery systems have changed a bit. For more information on other books (and resources) created from a biblical perspective, go to www.moodypublishers.com or write to:

Moody Publishers
820 N. LaSalle Boulevard
Chicago, IL 60610

3 5 7 9 10 8 6 4

Printed in the United States of America

Blessed is the man who has friends who are like brothers. More blessed is the man who has brothers who are also good friends. I am one such man, blessed with two older brothers who are also the closest of friends. I gratefully dedicate this book to one of those brothers, Greg Allen.

Contents

Introduction 9
1. The Conditions of Power in Prayer 13
2. Praying and Waiting 33
3. David's Dying Prayer 51
4. The Golden Key of Prayer 63
5. Prayer, the Proof of Godliness 77
6. Lead Us Not into Temptation 91
7. Pray Without Ceasing 113
8. Thanksgiving and Prayer 135

Acknowledgments 155

Introduction

BY JASON K. ALLEN

NEARLY 200 YEARS after his birth, Charles Spurgeon still stands as an icon on the evangelical landscape. His renown has proven global in reach and constant in endurance. Christians everywhere still speak of Spurgeon. Most who are familiar with church history know at least the broad contours of his life and ministry. Spurgeon was born in 1834 and lived and ministered in London, England, until his death in 1892. By age 19, he was pastoring one of the largest churches in London and was well on his way to accruing a global reputation and influence.

Known as the Prince of Preachers, Spurgeon, and his hero George Whitefield, are commonly regarded as the two greatest preachers of the English language. The theologian Carl F. H. Henry was right when he described Spurgeon as "one of evangelical Christianity's immortals."

But what made Spurgeon such a powerful preacher? What made the Metropolitan Tabernacle such a dynamic church?

On both counts, Spurgeon cited prayer as the secret to their success. Spurgeon pointed to prayer as the empowerment of his ministry and of his church. Every Monday night, congregants gathered in the auditorium for a prayer meeting, which, according to Spurgeon, was the secret of the church's power. Similarly, on Sundays, while Spurgeon preached, the Metropolitan Tabernacle basement teemed with church members praying for the worship service, the preaching of the Word of God, for the conversion of sinners, and for Spurgeon himself. Spurgeon occasionally took church visitors to the basement and would declare, "here is the powerhouse of the church."

Not only was Spurgeon buoyed by the prayers of others, he was devoted to prayer himself. After his first trip to London, the famed American evangelist D. L. Moody was asked if he had the privilege of hearing Spurgeon preach. Moody responded, "Yes, but better still I heard him pray." Though he was known as the Prince of Preachers, prayer is what catalyzed his spiritual fervency and ministerial impact. And it is prayer that will catalyze yours as well.

Whether in Spurgeon's day or in ours, the urge to hustle through prayer (or skip it altogether) in order to tackle our daily responsibilities is a temptation we all face. But in this regard, we can learn from Spurgeon, and I've compiled this book toward that end.

In this book, I've curated some of Charles Spurgeon's best, most helpful sermons on prayer and have packaged them for maximum accessibility and impact. No matter the weight of our burdens, the depths of our sorrows, the ambitions of our lives, the intensity of our fear, or the length of our to-do list, we must first pray. Pray and rest in Him.

May this book not only acquaint you with Spurgeon and his sermons on prayer, but may it acquaint you with how to pray more biblically, more faithfully, and, in the end, more effectively.

TITLE:

The Conditions of Power in Prayer

TEXT:

1 John 3:22–24

SUMMARY:

The essentials of the power of prayer are given: childlike obedience, childlike reverence, childlike trust, and childlike love. If there is prevalence of these essentials, our prayers will not be unprofitable. We look at our lives when approaching God and rely on His Spirit to direct our prayers.

NOTABLE QUOTES

"Whatever may have been your previous condition of life, if now penitently you seek the Lord's face, through the appointed Mediator, you will find Him."

"We believe that the prayers of Christians are a part of the machinery of providence, cogs in the great wheel of destiny, and when God leads His children to pray, He has already set in motion a wheel that is to produce the result prayed for, and the prayers offered are moving as a part of the wheel."

A sermon preached by Charles H. Spurgeon on March 22, 1873. *Metropolitan Tabernacle Pulpit*, vol. 19.

1

The Conditions of Power in Prayer

And whatever we ask we receive from Him, because we keep His commandments and do those things that are pleasing in His sight. And this is His commandment: that we should believe on the name of His Son Jesus Christ and love one another, as He gave us commandment. Now he who keeps His commandments abides in Him, and He in him. And by this we know that He abides in us, by the Spirit whom He has given us.

1 JOHN 3:22-24

I THOUGHT OF ADDRESSING YOU this morning on the importance of prayer, and I designed to stir you up to pray for me and the Lord's work in this place. Truly, I do not think I could have had a weightier subject or one that weighs more upon my soul. If I offered one request to you, it would be this: "pray for us." Of what use can our ministry be without the divine blessing, and how can we expect the divine blessing unless the church seeks it? I would say it even with tears: "pray for us." Be abundant in intercession, for only so can our prosperity as a church be increased or continued.

The question occurred to me: What if there is something in the church that would prevent our prayers being successful? That is a previous question that ought to be considered most earnestly even before we exhort you to pray. As Isaiah 1 teaches, the prayers of an unholy people soon become abominations to God. "When you spread out your hands, I will hide My eyes from you; Even though you make many prayers, I will not hear."

Churches may fall into such a state that their devotions will be an iniquity. Even the solemn meeting will weary the Lord. There may be evils in our hearts that may render it impossible for God to regard our intercessions. If we have iniquity in our hearts, the Lord will not hear us.

According to our text, some things are essential to prevalence in prayer. God will hear all true prayer, but there are certain things God's people must possess, or their prayers will fail. The text tells us, "whatever we ask we receive from Him, because we keep His commandments and do those things that are pleasing in His sight." Our subject is the essentials to power in prayer: what we must do, be, and have if we are to prevail habitually with God in prayer. Let us learn how to become Elijahs and Jacobs.

ESSENTIALS OF POWER IN PRAYER

We must make a few distinctions at the outset. There is a great difference between the prayer of a soul seeking mercy and the prayer of a saved person. If you sincerely seek mercy of God through Jesus Christ, you shall have it. Whatever may have been your previous condition of life, if now penitently you seek the Lord's face, through the appointed Mediator, you will find Him. If the Holy Spirit has taught you to pray, hasten to the cross and rest your guilty soul on Jesus.

We must speak in a different way to the saved. You have now become the people of God. While you will be heard and will daily find the grace every seeker receives in answer to prayer, you are now a child of God and thus under a special discipline as such. In that discipline, answers to prayer occupy a high position. There is something for a believer to enjoy over and above bare salvation: mercies, blessings, comforts, and favors that render his present life useful, happy, and honorable, though not irrespective of character. They are not matters of salvation, but these honors are given or withheld according to our obedience. If you neglect obedience, your heavenly Father will withhold these honors from you. The essential blessings of the covenant of grace stand unconditioned; the invitation to seek for mercy is addressed to everyone. But other choice blessings are given or withheld according to our attention to the Lord's rules in His family.

To give a common illustration: If a hungry person were at your door asking for bread, you would give it to him, whatever might be his character. You will also give your child food, whatever may be his behavior. You will not deny your child anything that is necessary for life, but there are many other things your child may desire that you will give him if he is obedient but will withhold if he is rebellious. This illustrates how far the paternal government of God will push this matter and where it will not go.

Understand also that the text refers not so much to God's hearing a prayer of His servants now and then, for that He will do even when His servants are out of course with Him and when He is hiding His face from them. The power in prayer here intended is continuous and absolute so that "whatever we ask we receive from Him."

Childlike Obedience

For this prayer, there are certain prerequisites and essentials, and the first is childlike obedience. If we are destitute of this, the Lord may say to us, "You have forsaken Me and served other gods. Therefore I will deliver you no more. Go and cry out to the gods which you have chosen" (Judg. 10:13–14).

Any father will tell you that granting the request of a disobedient child would encourage rebellion in the family and render it impossible for him to rule in his own house. The parent must often say, "My child, you did not listen to my word just now, and, therefore, I cannot listen to yours." It is not that the father does not love, but because of his love, he must show his displeasure by refusing the request of his erring offspring.

God acts with us as we should act toward our rebellious children, and if He sees that we will go into sin and transgress, it is part of His kind discipline to say, "I will shut out your prayer when you cry unto Me; I will not hear you when you entreat of Me; I will not destroy you, but you shall have no more of the luxuries of My kingdom or special prevalence with Me in prayer." That the Lord deals this way with His own people is clear from Psalm 81:13–16:

> "Oh, that My people would listen to Me,
> That Israel would walk in My ways!
> I would soon subdue their enemies,
> And turn My hand against their adversaries.
> The haters of the LORD would pretend submission to Him,
> But their fate would endure forever.
> He would have fed them also with the finest of wheat;
> And with honey from the rock I would have satisfied you."

Why, if the disobedient child of God had the promise put into his hands—"whatever things you ask in prayer, believing, you will receive" (Matt. 21:22)—he would ask for something that would bolster him up in his rebellion. This can never be tolerated. Shall God pander to our corruptions? Shall He find fuel for the flames of carnal passion? A self-willed heart hankers after greater liberty that it may be the more obstinate; a haughty spirit longs for greater elevation that it may be prouder still; a slothful spirit asks for greater ease that it may be yet more indolent; and a domineering spirit asks for more power that it may have more opportunities for oppression.

Shall God listen to such prayers as these? It cannot be. He will give us what we ask if we keep His commandments, but if we become disobedient, He also will reject prayers. Happy will we be if, through divine grace, we can say with David, "I will wash my hands in innocence; so I will go about Your altar, O LORD" (Ps. 26:6).

Childlike Reverence

Next to this is another essential to victorious prayer: childlike reverence. Notice the next sentence: We receive what we ask "because we keep His commandments and do those things that are pleasing in His sight."

We do not allow children to question the propriety or wisdom of their father's command; obedience ends where questioning begins. A child's standard of its duty must not become the measure of the father's right to command. The weightiest reason for a loving child's action is that it would please his parents, and the strongest thing that can be said to hold back a gracious child is that such a course of action would displease his parents. It is precisely so with us toward God, who is a perfect parent, and therefore we may without fear of mistake always make His pleasure the rule of right, while the rule of wrong may safely remain that which would displease Him.

Suppose any of us should be self-willed and say, "I shall not do what pleases God; I shall do what pleases myself." Then what would be the nature of our prayers? Our prayers might then be summed up in the request, "Let me have my own way." And can we expect God to consent to that? Would you have the Almighty resign the throne to place a proud mortal there? If you have a child in your house who has no respect for his father but who says, "I want to have my own way in all things," will you stoop to him? Will you allow him to dictate to you? God's house is not ordered so: He will not listen to His self-willed children, except to hear them in anger and answer them in wrath.

Remember how He heard the prayer of Israel for meat, and when the meat was in their mouths it became a curse to them (see Num. 11). Many persons are chastened by obtaining their own desires. We must have a childlike reverence of God so that we feel, "Lord, if what I ask for does not please You, neither would it please me. My desires are put into Your hands to be corrected. Strike the pen through every petition I offer that is not right, and put in whatever I have omitted. Good Lord, if I ought to have desired it, hear me as if I had desired it. 'Not as I will, but as You will.'"

This yielding spirit is essential to continual prevalence with God in prayer; the reverse is a sure bar to eminence in supplication. The Lord will be reverenced by those who are near Him. They must have an eye to His pleasure in all that they do and all that they ask, or He will not look upon them with favor.

Childlike Trust

In the third place, the text suggests the necessity of childlike trust: "And this is His commandment: that we should believe on the name of His Son Jesus Christ." Everywhere in Scripture, faith in God is spoken of as necessary to successful prayer. We must believe that God is and that He rewards those who diligently seek Him. The success of our prayer will be in proportion to our faith. It is a standing rule of the kingdom: "According to your faith let it be to you" (Matt. 9:29).

Remember how the Holy Spirit speaks through James: "If any of you lacks wisdom, let him ask of God, who gives to all liberally and without reproach, and it will be given to him.

But let him ask in faith, with no doubting, for he who doubts is like a wave of the sea driven and tossed by the wind. For let not that man suppose that he will receive anything from the Lord" (James 1:5–7). The text speaks of faith in the name of Jesus Christ, which means faith in His declared character, in His gospel, in the truth concerning His substitution and salvation. Or it may mean faith in the authority of Christ, so that when I say, "Do it in the name of Jesus," I mean, "Do for me as You would have done for Jesus."

He who prays with faith in the name cannot fail, for Jesus has said, "If you ask anything in My name, I will do it" (John 14:14). But there must be faith, and if there is no faith, we cannot expect to be heard. Do you not see that?

Let us come back to our family similitudes again. Suppose a child does not believe his father's word and is constantly saying that he doubts his father's truthfulness. Suppose he is not at all shocked that he should say such a thing, but he rather feels that he ought to be pitied, as if it were an infirmity which he could not avoid. He does not believe that his father speaks the truth, and he declares that, though he tries to believe his father's promise, he cannot. I think a father so basely distrusted would not be in a very great hurry to grant such a son's requests; indeed, it is very probable that the petitions of the mistrustful son would be such as could not be granted even if his father were willing to do so, since they would gratify his own unbelief and dishonor his parent.

For instance, suppose this child should doubt whether his father would provide him with his daily food. He might then say, "Father, give me enough money to last for the next ten years, for I shall then be a man and able to provide for myself. Give me money to quiet my fears, for I am in great anxiety." The father replies, "My son, what should I do that for?" And he gets for a reply, "I am very sorry to say it, dear father, but I cannot trust you; I have such a weak faith in you and your love that I am afraid one of these days you will leave me to starve, and therefore I should like to have something sure in the bank." Which of you fathers would listen to this child's request? You would feel grieved that thoughts so dishonoring should pass through the mind of your child, and you would not—and could not—give way to them.

Apply the parable to yourselves. Did you offer requests of the same character? You have been unable to trust God to provide your daily bread, and therefore you have been craving for what you call "some provision for the future." You want a more trusty provider than providence, a better security than God's promise. You are unable to trust your heavenly Father's word! In a thousand ways we insult the Lord by imagining "the things which are seen" to be more substantial than His unseen omnipotence.

We ask God to give us at once what we do not require at present, and may never need at all, because we distrust Him. Brethren, are you not to blame here, and do you expect the Lord to aid and abet your folly? Shall God pander to your distrust? Shall He give you a heap of cankering gold and silver for thieves to steal and chests of garments to feed moths? Would you have the Lord act as if He admitted the correctness of your suspicions and confessed to unfaithfulness? God forbid! Expect not, therefore, to be heard when your prayer is suggested by an unbelieving heart: "Commit your way to the LORD, trust also in Him, and He shall bring it to pass" (Ps. 37:5).

Childlike Love

The next essential to continued success in prayer is childlike love: "That we should believe on the name of His Son Jesus Christ and love one another, as He gave us commandment." The great commandment after faith is love. As it is said of God, "God is love," so may we say that "Christianity is love." If we were each one incarnations of love, we should have attained to the complete likeness of Christ.

We should abound in love to God, Christ, the church, sinners, and men everywhere. When a man has no love to God, he is like a child without love to his father. Shall his father promise absolutely to fulfill all the desires of his unloving heart? Or if a child has no love to his brothers and sisters, shall the father trust him with an absolute promise, and say, "Ask and it shall be given to you"? Why, the unloving son would impoverish the whole family by his selfish demands; regardless of all the rest of the household, he would only care to indulge his own passions. He would soon seek the kingdom for himself.

Selfishness cannot be trusted with power in prayer. Unloving spirits cannot be trusted with great, broad, unlimited promises. If God is to hear us, we must love God and each other. For when we love God, we shall not pray for anything that would not honor God and shall not wish to see anything

The Conditions of Power in Prayer

happen that would not also bless our brethren. You must get rid of selfishness before God can trust you with the keys of heaven, but when self is dead, then He will enable you to unlock His treasures.

We must have childlike ways as well: "he who keeps His commandments abides in Him, and He in him." It is one of a child's ways to love his home. The good child to whose requests his father always listens loves no place so much as the house where his parents live. Now he who loves and keeps God's commandments dwells in Him—he has made the Lord his dwelling. He has become like God, and now his prayers are such as God can answer.

To dwell in God is needful to power with God. Suppose one of you had a boy who said, "Father, I do not like my home, I do not care for you, and I will not endure the restraints of family rule; I am going to live with strangers, but I shall come to you every week, and I shall require many things of you, and I expect you to give me whatever I ask." You will say, "My son, how can you speak to me in such a manner? If you utterly disregard me, can you expect me to support you in your cruel unkindness and wicked insubordination? No, my son, if you will not remain with me and own me as a father, I cannot promise you anything." And so it is with God.

If we will dwell with Him, He will give us all things. If we love Him as He should be loved and trust Him as He ought to be trusted, then He will hear our requests. But if not, it is unreasonable to expect it. Indeed, it would be a slur upon the divine character to fulfill unholy desires and gratify evil whims.

He may give you the bread and water of affliction, but certainly He will not give you what your heart desires.

One thing more: we must have a childlike spirit, for "by this we know that He abides in us, by the Spirit whom He has given us." What is this but the Spirit of adoption—the Spirit that rules in all the children of God? The willful who think and feel and act differently from God must not expect that God will come round to their way of thinking and feeling and acting. The Holy Spirit, if He rules in us, will subordinate our nature to His own sway, and then the prayers that spring out of our renewed hearts will be in keeping with the will of God, and such prayers will naturally be heard.

No parent would think of listening to a willful child. Shall God grant us that which we ask for when it is contrary to His holy mind? Such a possibility is not conceivable. The same mind must be in us that was also in Christ Jesus, and then we shall be able to say, "I know that You hear me always."

THE PREVALENCE OF THESE ESSENTIALS

First, if we have faith in God, there is no question about God's hearing our prayer. If we can plead in faith the name and blood of Jesus, we must obtain answers of peace. But a thousand cavils are suggested. Suppose these prayers concern the laws of nature, then the scientific men are against us. What of that? I do not know of any prayer worth praying that does not come into contact with some natural law or other, and yet I believe in prayers being heard.

Some say God will not change the laws of nature for us, and I reply, "Whoever said He would!" The Lord has ways of answering our prayers irrespective of the working of miracles or suspending laws. He used to hear prayer by miracle, but as I have often said to you, that seems a rougher way of achieving His purpose; it is like stopping a vast machine for a small result, but He knows how to accomplish His ends and hear our prayers by I know not what secret means. Perhaps there are other forces and laws which He has arranged to bring into action just at times when prayer also acts, laws just as fixed, and forces just as natural as those our learned theorizers have discovered. The wisest men know not all the laws that govern the universe, nay, nor a tithe of them.

We believe that the prayers of Christians are a part of the machinery of providence, cogs in the great wheel of destiny, and when God leads His children to pray, He has already set in motion a wheel that is to produce the result prayed for, and the prayers offered are moving as a part of the wheel. If there be but faith in God, God must either cease to be or cease to be true, or else He must hear prayer.

Confidence in God

The verse before the text says, "If our heart does not condemn us, we have confidence toward God. And whatever we ask we receive from Him." He who has a clear conscience comes to God with confidence, and that confidence of faith ensures the answer of his prayer. Childlike confidence makes us pray as none else can. I have often felt that it needs more confidence in God to pray to Him about a little thing than about great things. We fancy that our great things are somewhat worthier of God's regard, though in truth they are little enough to Him, and then we imagine that our little things must be so trifling that it would be almost an insult to bring them before Him. But we should know that what is very great to a child may be very little to his parent, and yet the parent measures the thing from the child's point of view. God our Father is a good Father; He pities us as fathers pity their children and condescends to us. He tells the number of the stars and calls them by name, yet He heals the brokenhearted and binds up their wounds. If you have confidence in God, you will take your great things and your little things to Him, and He will never belie your confidence. Faith must succeed.

Love Must Succeed

But next, love must succeed too, since we have already seen that the man who loves in the Christian sense is in accord with God. If you confine your love to your own family, you must not expect God to do so, and prayers narrowed within that circle He will disregard. If a man loves his own little self and hopes everybody's crop of wheat will fail, he certainly cannot expect the Lord to agree with such selfishness. If a man has heart enough to embrace all the creatures of God in his affection, while he yet prays specially for the household of faith, his prayers will be after the divine mind. His love and God's goodness run side by side. Though God's love is like a mighty rolling river, and his is like a trickling brooklet, they both run in the same direction and will come to the same end. God always hears the prayers of a loving man because those prayers are the shadows of His own decrees.

Again, God will hear the man of obedience because his obedient heart leads him to pray humbly and with submission, for his highest desire is that the Lord's will be done. Hence his prayers are prophecies. Is he not one with God? Doth he not desire and ask for exactly what God intends? How can a prayer shot from such a bow ever fail to reach its target?

The difficulty is that we do not keep in rapport with God; but if we did, then we should strike the same note as God strikes—the note struck by prayer on earth would coincide with that which sounds forth from the decrees in heaven. Again, the man who lives in fellowship with God will assuredly begin praying, because if he dwells in God, and God dwells in him, he will desire what God desires.

And here, again, let us say, our text speaks of the Christian man as being filled with God's Spirit: "By this we know that He abides in us, by the Spirit whom He has given us." Who knows the mind of a man but the spirit of a man? So, who knows the things of God but the Spirit of God? And if the Spirit of God dwells in us, then He tells us what God's mind is; He makes intercession in the saints according to God's will.

It is sometimes imagined that men who have prevalence in prayer can pray for what they like, but I can assure you any one of these will tell you that that is not so. You may call upon such a man and ask him to pray for you, but he cannot promise that he will. There are strange holdings back to such men, when they feel, they know not how or why, that they cannot pray effectual fervent prayers in certain cases, though they might desire to do so. God gives a discretion, a judgment, and a wisdom, and the Spirit makes intercession in the saints according to the will of God.

PRACTICAL APPLICATIONS

Thus I think I have laid down the doctrine pretty clearly. Now a few minutes of practical improvement, as the old Puritans used to say. I only wish it may be of improvement to many of us.

The first is, we want to pray for a great blessing as a church. I think I should command your suffrages if I said we intend to pray God to send a blessing on the church at large. Very well. Have we the essentials for success? Are we believing in the name of Jesus Christ? Are we full of love to God and one another?

The double commandment is that we believe on the name of Jesus Christ and that we love one another. Do we love one another? Are we walking in love? None of us are perfect in it. I will begin to confess by acknowledging I am not what I should be in that respect. Will you let the confession go round, and each one think how often we have done unloving things and thought unloving things and said unloving things and listened to unloving gossip and held back our hand unlovingly when we ought to have rendered help and put forth our hand unlovingly to push down a man who was falling? If in the church of God there is a lack of love, we cannot expect prayer to be heard. Do you expect God to save sinners whom you do not love, and to convert souls whom you do not care a bit about? We must love souls into Christ, for, under God's Holy Spirit, the great instrument for the conquest of the world is love, and if Christians will love more than Muslims do and Jews do, they will overcome Muslims and Jews, and if they show less love, Muslims and Jews will overcome them.

Next, are we doing that which is pleasing in God's sight? We cannot expect answers to prayer if we are not. Put the enquiry to yourselves all round. Let each church member answer that question. Have you been doing lately that which you would like Jesus Christ to see? Correct yourself. Unless the members of God's church do that which is pleasing in His sight, they bar the door against prosperity; they prevent the prayers of the church from succeeding.

The next question is, do we dwell in God? I mean, during the day, do we think of God? A Christian is not to run unto God in the morning, and again at night, and use Him as a shelter and a makeshift, as people do of an arch or a portico, which they run under in a shower of rain, but we are to dwell in God and live in Him, from the rising of the sun until the going down thereof, making Him our daily meditation and walking as in His sight.

Last, does the Spirit of God actuate us, or is it another spirit? Do we wait upon God and say, "Lord, let your Spirit tell me what to say in this case, and what to do; rule my judgment, subdue my passions, keep down my baser impulses, and let your Spirit guide me"? Let us pray God to make the wheat be the stronger. One of two things always happens in a church.

Either the wheat chokes the weeds, or the weeds choke the wheat. God grant that the wheat may overtop the weeds in our case. God grant grace to His servants to be strong enough to overcome the evil that surrounds them, and, having done all, to stand to the praise of the glory of His grace, who also has made us accepted in the Beloved. The Lord bless you and be with you evermore. Amen and amen.

TITLE:
Praying and Waiting

TEXT:
1 John 5:13–15

SUMMARY:
Spurgeon wants to strengthen his people to look for answers to prayer. Spurgeon first offers an explanation and gives case studies from the Old Testament on saints expecting answers to their prayers. Spurgeon then gives a commendation for seeking answer to prayer. We honor God in expecting an answer to prayer. We honor His attributes and truthfulness. Spurgeon then gives a rebuke to those who pray but do not expect an answer. Spurgeon concludes by giving an exhortation to expectations of answer to prayer.

NOTABLE QUOTES

"He who prays without expecting to receive a return mocks at the mercy seat of God."

"Let your sense of the poverty of your prayers lead you to abhor your faults but not to abhor praying."

"May I beseech you by the love you bear to Jesus, do Him the honor of believing in the prevalence of His plea."

A sermon preached by Charles H. Spurgeon on October 23, 1864. *Metropolitan Tabernacle Pulpit*, vol. 10.

2

Praying and Waiting

These things I have written to you who believe in the name of the Son of God, that you may know that you have eternal life, and that you may continue to believe in the name of the Son of God. Now this is the confidence that we have in Him, that if we ask anything according to His will, He hears us. And if we know that He hears us, whatever we ask, we know that we have the petitions that we have asked of Him.

1 JOHN 5:13–15

JOHN ADDRESSES HIMSELF to those who have believed on the Son of God, laboring to conduct them up three glorious ascents of the mount of God.

THE THREE ASCENTS

The Full Assurance of Faith

The first ascent he would have them take is from faith to the full assurance of faith. He writes to them as believers, "These things I have written to you who believe in the name of the Son of God, that you may know that you have eternal life." As believers, they had eternal life, but it is one thing to have eternal life and another to know that we have eternal life. A man may know Christ in his heart, and yet at certain seasons, he may be cast into doubts as to whether he has any saving knowledge of the Lord Jesus at all.

I know there are some who do not like us to draw any distinction between faith and assurance, but the more I think upon the subject, the more I am compelled to do it, not for the encouragement of unbelief but for the consolation of those weaklings of the flock, whose faith has not ripened into assurance. Believers who have observed their own experience must have noticed that even when they can cast themselves in all simplicity upon Christ Jesus, yet even then they cannot at all times enjoy the comfortable persuasion of security, because their minds are distracted, and Satan has gained an advantage over them. They trust their God, but it is with something of the spirit of Job when he said, "Though He slay me, yet will I trust Him."

Even the strongest of saints must observe that, while always believing, they are not always assured. This must certainly be the case with the weaker ones and the beginners. I know faith is a sureness concerning the truth of God. I cheerfully accept the definition but must bid you observe that there is a difference between being sure of the truth of God and being sure that I am a partaker of divine life. I come to Christ not knowing whether He died especially for me, or no; but I trust in Him as the Savior of sinners: this is faith.

But having trusted in Him, I discover that I have a particular and special interest in the merit of His blood and in the love of His heart: this is rather assurance than faith. Although assurance will grow out of faith, the two are not identical. You may believe in Christ and have eternal life, and still be in doubt about it; you ought not to be, but still you may fall into such a state. The apostle desires that if you believe, you may come to a still higher state and may infallibly and joyfully know that you have eternal life. Continue to rest in Jesus, and you shall find that in Him, as you have attained faith, you shall also obtain an assurance of faith. Here is the first heavenly staircase.

The Power of Prayer

From the assurance of our interest in Christ, the next step is to a firm belief in the power of prayer: "Now this is the confidence that we have in Him, that if we ask anything according to His will, He hears us." My belief in the prevalence of my prayer, to a great extent, must depend upon my conviction of my interest in Christ.

For instance, here is Paul's argument: "He who did not spare His own Son, but delivered Him up for us all, how shall He not with Him also freely give us all things?" (Rom. 8:32).

I must therefore be sure that God has given me Christ, and if He has given Christ to me, then I know that He will give me all things. But if I have any doubt about Christ's being mine and about my being the receiver of God's unspeakable gift in Christ, I cannot reason as the apostle did, and I cannot therefore have that confidence that my prayer is heard.

God's fatherhood is another ground of our confidence in prayer. If I am not clear that God is my Father, then I cannot come to God with confidence that He will give me my desire. My sonship being assured, I am confident that my Father knows what I need and will hear me, but my sonship being in dispute, my power in prayer vanishes. Besides, the man who has faith in Christ has already received answers to prayer, and answers to prayer are some of the best supports to our faith as to the future success of our petitions. But if I have no reason to conclude that God has heard my prayer for forgiveness, how can I come with confidence? No, brothers and sisters, seek in the first place, since you have believed in Jesus, to get the witness within you that you are born of God, and then go from this gracious ascent to the next, knowing and being assured that He hears us always because we do the things that please Him and plead the name of our Lord Jesus Christ who is all in all to us.

God Answers Prayer

If you have climbed this second ascent, the third is not difficult. It is to go from your belief that God hears prayer to a conviction that when you have desired anything of God in prayer, through Jesus Christ, you have obtained the answer.

We have heaven, but we have it not in enjoyment as yet, and so we may have answers to our prayers, and yet as far as our sense is concerned, we may not have received anything. We have it, but we see it not; it is ours, but our God sees fit to reserve it for a season for a further trial of our faith. If a man had nothing more than he could see, his estate would be sorely diminished. So we may have the answer to many of our prayers, really have the answer, and yet for the present that answer is unseen. May we, dear friends, obtain the gracious position of knowing that having sought the Lord in prayer through Jesus Christ, we have the petitions we desired of Him.

Seeing that you have the promise of an answer to prayer, and that the answer must come to you, look for it. Unless you believe that you have the answer in reality, you are not likely to watch for its appearance; but if you have come so far as to believe that you have the answer, I do now earnestly urge you to look for it and rejoice.

EXPLANATION OF PRAYER

Elijah bowed his knee on the top of Carmel and prayed to God for rain. For three years there had not been a single drop descending upon Israel. He pleads, and having finished his intercession, he says to his servant, "Go up now, look toward the sea" (1 Kings 18:43). He did not think it sufficient to have prayed; he believed that he had the petition he desired of God, and therefore he sent his servant to see. The answer brought back was not encouraging, but he said to his servant, "Go again" seven times, and seven times that servant went.

Elijah does not appear to have staggered in his faith; he believed he had the petition and therefore expected soon to see it. He sent his servant till at last he brought back the news, "There is a cloud, as small as a man's hand, rising out of the sea!" Quite enough for Elijah's faith. He goes down to tell Ahab to make ready his chariot that the rain stops him not.

David is another case in point. Let me quote but this one expression, "My voice You shall hear in the morning, O Lord; In the morning I will direct it to You, And I will look up" (Ps. 5:3). As men take an arrow from the quiver, so David takes his prayer and directs it to God. He is not shooting to the right hand or to the left but upwards to his God. Anxious to know how it speeds, he looks up to see whether the Lord accepts his desire and continues to look up to see whether a gracious answer is returned. This is what I mean by the Christian's knowing he has an answer to his petition and waiting and watching till it comes.

Take the case of poor, strong, yet weak Samson: as strong in faith as he was in body. After his hair had grown again, he is brought to make sport for the Philistines, and he prays to God to strengthen him but this once. Mark how he believed he had the petition, for he said to the man who conducted him blindfolded into the Philistines' temple, "Let me feel the pillars which support the temple, so that I can lean on them." And why does he seek to stand there? Because he believes he has his petition. See how in the strength of his belief he pulls down the temple of Dagon about the heads of the worshipers and proves the power of believing supplication!

Take again, the case of Hannah, a woman of a sorrowful spirit. She prayed without an audible voice, only her lips moved. As soon as Eli told her that God had heard the prayer, observe the change wrought in her: "her face was no longer sad." The man of God has said it, and that is enough for her. The wrinkles disappear from her brow and the tears from her eye.

A yet more wonderful instance is that of Jacob, who not only believes in the utility of prayer, but he will not let the angel depart till he wins the blessing of him. This was going further: not only believing that there was a blessing and that prayer could get it, but a determination not to cease prayer till he had some visible token that he had obtained it. Here was strong faith. The case may be exceptional, and especially when we pray for temporal mercies, though there may be times when we say unto the covenant angel, "I will not leave this closet till you give me your answer."

I have to complain of myself, and I suppose you must complain in the same manner, that so much of our prayer is lacking here. We do not send the servant to look to the sea; we do not let our countenance grow glad when we have poured out our hearts before God. This is base and wicked of us.

COMMENDATION OF PRAYER

Let me commend the habit of expecting an answer to prayer and looking for it. By this means, you honor upon God's ordinance of prayer. He who prays without expecting to receive a return mocks at the mercy seat of God. For of what use is the mercy seat if God has said, "Seek my face" in vain? If no answers come to supplication, then supplication is a vain waste of time. You play with prayer when you do not expect an answer. The truly prayerful man is resolved in his own soul that he must have the answer.

Such a spirit also honors God's attributes. To believe that the Lord will hear my prayer honors His truthfulness. He has said that He will, and I believe He will keep His word. It honors His power. I believe that He can make the word of His mouth stand fast. It honors His love. The larger things I ask, the more do I honor the liberality, grace, and love of God in asking such great things. It honors His wisdom, for if I ask what He has told me to ask and expect Him to answer me, I believe that His word is wise and may safely be kept.

Christian brother, let me commend the gracious art of believing in the success of your prayer because in this way, you will help to insure your own success. Furthermore, thus to believe in the result of prayer tries and manifests faith. Perhaps nine prayers out of ten that we offer might have been as well unoffered, for any good they have done to us. Am I too severe? I mean our hurried morning prayer; I mean our sleepy evening prayers; I mean those formal petitions in which you have only expressed godly opinions without feeling godly emotions, passed over holy words without their really coming from your hearts.

But when we pray and expect the answer, this is a sure token that our prayer has not been a mere formality. Then Faith lays hold upon God, and she waits, Patience standing by her side, knowing that the windows of heaven will open soon, and

God's right hand will scatter His liberality upon waiting souls. So Faith waits and watches, and waits and watches again. This is the reason why the glorious doctrine of the second advent has such a blessed effect on some of God's people. It exercises their faith and brings hope into the field. The devil says, "Surely God will never hear your prayer." You answer, "I have the petition, and am waiting till He puts it into my hand; it is up there, labeled for me and set aside in the treasury for me, and I shall have it. I am waiting till the time comes when I may safely receive that which is mine even now."

So the flesh whispers, "It is in vain." But Faith says, "No, prayer is blessed, prayer is God's Spirit returning whence it came, and it will never fail." "But how can such a sinner as you are hope to succeed with God?" whispers Unbelief. But Faith keeps on waiting still till it gets its reward.

Such a habit, moreover, helps to bring out our gratitude to God. None sing so sweetly as those who get answers to prayer. Oh! Some of you would give my Master sweet songs if you did but notice when He hears you, but perhaps the Lord may drop an answer to your prayer, and you merely cry, "It is a fortunate circumstance," and God gets no praise for it. But if, instead, you had been watching for it, and saw it come, you would fall on your knees in holy gratitude, and say,

> I love the Lord: He heard my cries,
> And pitied every groan:
> Long as I live, when troubles rise,
> I'll hasten to His throne.

I will not say more, lest by multiplying commendations I rather weaken the force of what I say. I could not praise this habit too much. The man whom God has taught to pray believingly has all God's treasures at his command. You have the privy key of the Lord's secret cabinet. You are rich to all the extents of bliss. You have about you the omnipotence of God, for you have power to move the arm that moves the world. He who lacks this mercy is but weak and poverty stricken, but he who has gained it is one of the mightiest in God's Israel and will do great exploits.

A GENTLE REBUKE

Having thus spoken by way of commendation, we pause awhile to speak by way of rebuke, but it shall be such a gentle rebuke as shall not break the head.

I am not just now speaking to those who never pray at all; let me, however, solemnly remind them that prayerless souls are Christless souls and will be lost souls ere long. Nor am I speaking to those of you who merely prattle through a form of prayer. I give you but this one word: God will not forever be mocked by you, and your prayers are numbered with your sins. You insult the majesty of heaven while you pretend to worship.

I am communing this morning with those who believe on the name of the Son of God and in the efficacy of prayer. How do you not expect an answer? I think I hear you say, "One reason is my own unworthiness; how can I think that God will hear such prayers as mine?" Brother, let me remind you that it is not the man who prays that commends the prayer to God but the fervency of the prayer and the virtue of the great Intercessor.

Did you ever read Psalm 34 and carefully consider where David was when his prayer had such good speed with God? He says, "O, magnify the LORD with me, and let us exalt His name together. I sought the LORD, and He heard me, And delivered me from all my fears. . . . This poor man cried out, and the LORD heard him." Now where do you think David prayed that prayer? Read the heading of the psalm: "A psalm of David, when he pretended madness before Abimelech, who drove him away, and he departed." You recollect what he did. He played the madman and let his spittle down his beard, acted the fool and was never more a fool—except once—than he was then. And yet, even then in his fool's play, God heard his prayer.

There is something very teaching here. You, child of God, though you may have gone ever so far astray and played the fool, let not this keep you back from the mercy seat; it was built on purpose for unworthy sinners to come to. You are such. If God did not hear you except in your good times, why then you would perish. The gates of His grace are open at night as well as at day, and sinning saints may come and find mercy as well as those who have kept their garments white. Do not, I pray you, get into the ill habit of judging that your prayers are not heard because of your failings in spirit.

"Yes," says a third, "it is not merely that I do not so much doubt the efficacy of prayer on account of myself, but my prayers themselves are such poor things. I cannot get the fervency I want. I cannot get to God; I do not know how to lay hold upon Him and wrestle with Him, and therefore I cannot expect to prevail." Dear brother, this is your sin as well as your infirmity. Be humbled and pray for God to make you like the importunate widow, for so only will you prevail.

But at the same time let me remind you that if your prayers are sincere, it shall often happen that even their weakness shall not destroy them. When Christ was asleep in the ship, His disciples came to Him and said, "Teacher, do You not care that we are perishing?" and He rebuked them: "How is it that you have no faith?" But He did not refuse to hear their cry for all that, for He rebuked the winds and the waves, and there was a great calm. He may rebuke the unbelief of your prayer, and yet in infinite mercy He may exceed His promise.

There is no promise that He will hear unbelieving prayers, and he who wavers must not expect to receive anything, but the Lord may go beyond His Word and give us mercies notwithstanding that fault. Let your sense of the poverty of your prayers lead you to abhor your faults but not to abhor praying. Let it make you long to pray better but never cause you to doubt that if you can with true fervency come to God through Jesus Christ your Lord, your prevailing is not a matter of hope but a matter of certainty, your success is as absolutely sure as the laws of nature.

Further, I have no doubt many of God's people cannot think their prayers will be heard because they have had as yet such few manifest replies. I saw the other day a greyhound coursing a hare. The moment the hare ran through the hedge out of the greyhound's sight, the race was over, for he could not follow where he could not see. The true hound hunts by scent but the greyhound only by sight. Now there are some Christians too much like the greyhound; they only follow the Lord as far as they can see His manifest mercy. But the true child of God hunts by faith. You say you have had no answers! How do you know? God may have answered you, though you have not seen the answer.

This is a riddle, but it is a fact. God has not promised to give you the particular mercy in kind, but He will give it you somehow or other. If I pay my debts in gold, no man can blame me because I do not pay them in silver; and if God gives you spiritual mercies in abundance, instead of temporal, He has heard your prayer. Christ prayed that God might hear Him; He was heard in that He feared, but He had not the cup taken from Him. No, but He had an angel to comfort and strengthen Him; and this was in truth an answer, though not such as the prayer seemed to require. You have had an answer, and if God has heard you but once, pluck up courage and go again.

Many do not pray expecting an answer because they pray in such a sluggish spirit. Begging is a hard trade; a man that succeeds in it must throw his heart into it, and so is praying; if you want to win, you must pray hard. They called some of the early Christians on the Continent, "Beg-hards," because they did pray hard to God; and none can prevail but those who pray hard. Slothful souls may not expect an answer.

Then there are so many, again, who pray in a legal spirit. Children of God know it is their duty to pray, but they pray because they believe in the efficacy of prayer. I should not expect God to hear me because the clock struck such and I began to pray from a sense of duty. No, I must go not because the clock strikes but because my heart wants to pray. A child does not cry because the time to cry has come, nor does a sick man groan because it is the hour of groaning, but they cry and groan because they cannot help it. A legal spirit would prevent expecting answers to prayer.

Inconsistences after prayer, and a failure to press our suit, will bring us to doubt the power of prayer. If we do not plead with God again and again and again, we shall not keep up our faith that God hears us. "Oh!" says one, "we have no time to pray at that rate." What do you do with your time? What shall be thought of us when we confess that we have no time to pray, but there is time for trifles! Princes of the blood royal and yet no time to be at court! Kings of a divine race and yet no time to put on your crowns and wear your robes of state! Time to play with toys and roll in the dust with the beggars of earth but no time to sit upon the throne of glory and to offer the sacrifice of praise unto the Most High! Shame on such Christians! May God give us true shame for this, and henceforth may we be much in prayer and expect gracious answers.

EXHORTATION TO PRAY

Dear friends, let us believe in God's answering prayer. Is He a God, and can He lie? Have we promise upon promise, and will He break them all? God forbid. Brethren, if there be a God, and if this Book be His Word, if God be true, prayer must be answered; and let us on our knees go to the sacred engagement as to a work of real efficacy.

Again, prayer must be answered because of the character of God our Father. Will He let His children cry and not hear them? He hears the young ravens, and will He not hear His own people? He is a God of love. Would you let your sick child lie and pine, and not go in to answer their groanings? Will a God of love fast close His ears against His people's cries? Do you think He will let the tears stream down your cheeks when you are petitioning and not put them into His bottle? Oh! Remember His lovingkindness, and you cannot, I think, doubt that He hears prayer. Do not rob Him of His character by distrusting Him.

Think of the efficacy of the blood of Jesus. When you pray, it is the blood that speaks. Every drop of Jesus's blood cries, "Father, hear him! Father, hear him! Hear the sinner's cry!" That blood was sprinkled on the mercy seat that the mercy seat might be efficacious for you. Do not doubt the blood of Christ. What! Can He die, and yet that blood have no more efficacy than the blood of bulls or of goats? You will not think this. Then do not doubt that prayer prevails.

Think again that Jesus pleads. He points to the wound upon His breast and spreads His pierced hands. Shall the Father deny the Son? Shall prayers offered by Christ be cast out from heaven's register? Oh! These things must not—cannot—be.

Besides, the Holy Spirit Himself is the author of your prayers. Will God invite the desire, and then not hear it? Shall there be a schism between the Father and the Holy Spirit? You will not dream of such a thing.

We have not the time to give instances in proof, but I hope your own experience furnishes them. May I beseech you by the love you bear to Jesus, do Him the honor of believing in the prevalence of His plea. By the light and life you have received of the Holy Ghost, do not discredit Him by thinking He can teach you to pray a prayer that will not be accepted before God.

Let us as a church pray more. Oh, that the spirit of prayer would come down upon us! Let us expect greater blessings. Let us stand on our watchtower and look. Let us meet again and again at special meetings, and let us cry mightily unto the Most High, pouring out our hearts like water before Him, and He will open the windows of heaven and give us greater blessings than we have ever had before, great as those already received have been. This very afternoon let the season of prayer begin, and let it be well sustained. It is to believers that these words are spoken. May God lead you who are not believers to trust in Jesus. Amen.

TITLE:
David's Dying Prayer

TEXT:
Psalm 72:19

SUMMARY:
Spurgeon's main goal is to have his people desire prayer. He begins by an *explanation* of the prayer. Spurgeon explains the call for the world to be filled with true Christianity. Spurgeon then aims to *spur people up to desire the thing for which David prayed*. This includes contemplating the majesty of God. Spurgeon gives *counsel for pursuit of this object*. He explains the need for the heart to be pure before someone prays for the earth to be filled with the glory of God.

NOTABLE QUOTES

"You cannot bow before God yourself and adore Him without wishing that all the rest of mankind should do the same."

"Beloved, we will wait awhile. We will still continue on this side with our Master; for though we are fighters now, we shall be winners by and by."

A sermon preached by Charles H. Spurgeon on April 26, 1857. *New Park Street Pulpit*, vol. 3.

3

David's Dying Prayer

*Let the whole earth be filled with His glory.
Amen and Amen.*

PSALM 72:19

THERE WAS A TIME when this prayer would have been unnecessary; a period, in fact, when it could not have been offered, seeing the thing to be asked for was already in being. A time there was when the word *rebellion* had not been uttered against the great magistracy of heaven; a day there was when the slime of sin had never been left by the trail of the serpent, for no serpent then existed, and no evil spirit. There was an hour, never to be forgotten, when the seraph might have flapped his wing for aye and never have found aught of discord or aught of rebellion or of anarchy throughout God's universe, when the mighty angels assembled in the halls of the Most High, and without exception did reverence to their liege Lord and paid Him homage due, when the vast creation revolved around its center, the great metropolis, the throne of God, and paid its daily and hourly homage unto Him, when the harmonies of creation always came to one spot and found their focus near the throne of God.

There was a time when every star was bright, when all space was filled with loveliness; when holiness, purity, and happiness were like a robe which mantled the entire creation. This world itself was once fair and lovely—so fair and lovely that we who live in these erring times can scarcely guess its beauty. It was the house of song and the dwelling place of praise. If it had no preeminence among its sister spheres, certainly it was inferior to none of them, surrounded with beauty, girt with gladness, and having in it holy and heavenly inhabitants. It was a house to which the angels themselves loved to resort, where the holy spirits, the morning stars, delighted to sing together over this beautiful and fair earth of ours. But now, how changed! How different! Now it is our duty devoutly to bend our knees and pray that the whole earth may yet be filled with His glory.

In one sense this prayer is still unnecessary, for in a certain sense the whole earth is filled with God's glory. But David intended this prayer in another sense, not as Creator, but as a moral Governor and a Ruler. It is as Governor that we have revolted from God and dishonored Him; it is as our Master, our Ruler, and our Judge that we have trampled on His crown. It is, therefore, in this respect that David wished that the whole earth might be filled with God's glory. A foolish wish, say you, for it never can be accomplished. Surely the day will never come when hoary systems of superstition shall die.

What! Shall colossal systems of infidelity and of idolatry totter to their fall? They have resisted the battering ram for many a year; and yet shall they pass away, and shall God's kingdom come, and His will be done on earth, even as it is in heaven? Nay, it is no daydream of a boy; it is no wish of the enthusiast. Mark who uttered that prayer, and where he was when he uttered it. It was the prayer of a dying king; it was the prayer of a holy man of God, whose eyes were just then lighted up with brightness in view of the celestial city. He uttered this as his last best wish and desire; and when he had uttered it, he sank back in his bed and said, "The prayers of David the son of Jesse are ended." It was his last prayer: "Let the whole earth be filled with His glory. Amen and Amen."

THE PRAYER EXPLAINED

It is a large prayer—a massive one. A prayer for a city needs a stretch of faith, ay, there are times when a prayer for one man is enough to stagger our belief; for we can scarcely think that God will hear us for even that one. But how great this prayer is, how comprehensive! It does not exempt one single country, however trodden under the foot of superstition; it does not leave out one single nation, however abandoned. For the cannibal as well as for the civilized, for the man who grasps the tomahawk as well as for the man who bends his knee in supplication, this prayer is uttered, "Let the whole earth be filled with His glory. Amen and Amen."

The psalmist desired that the true religion of God might be

sent into every country. Yes, it is a great prayer, but we mean it. We are praying against every form and fashion of false religion. We are crying against anti-Christ, and we are praying that the day may come when every temple shall be dismantled, when every shrine shall be left poor as poverty, and when there shall be no temple but the temple of the Lord God of Hosts, and when no song shall be sung but the song of Hallelujah; unto Him that loved us and washed us from our sins in His own blood.

But we mean more than this. We ask not merely for the nominal Christianity of any country but for the conversion of every family in every country. "Let the whole earth be filled with His glory. Amen and Amen." Is that wish too great, too high? Are we too sanguine in our expectations? No. We do not wish to see dry places here and there, but as the deep foundations of the depths are covered with the sea, so we wish that every nation may be covered with God's truth. And so we pray that every family may receive it; yes, we pray that every household may have its morning and its evening prayer; we pray that every family may be brought up in the fear of the Lord, that every child may, on its mother's knee, say, "Our Father," and that the answer may come to the infant's prayer, "Thy kingdom come."

But we go further than that. We do not ask merely for household conversion but for the individual salvation of every being existing. Should there be one heart that does not beat in God's praise, or one lip that is dumb in the melody of thanksgiving, then there would be yet a spot left which would not be filled with God's praise, and that one left unconverted would blot and blur the whole great work of filling the earth with God's glory. The salvation of one soul is unutterably precious, and when we offer this prayer, we exclude none. We pray that the atheist, the blasphemer, the hardened rebel, the profligate may each be filled with God's glory. This I believe to be the psalmist's prayer—that every man might be converted, and that in fact everywhere, in every heart and conscience, God might reign without a rival, Lord paramount over the great wide world.

ENFLAMED TO PRAY THIS PRAYER

I am going, in the second place, to try to stir you up to desire this great, this wonderful thing for which David prayed.

First, I beseech you, contemplate the majesty of God; or rather, since I am unable to help you to do that just now, let me remind you of seasons when you have in some measure grasped the thought of His divinity. Have you never at night gazed upon the starry orbs with the thought that God was the Maker of them all until your soul was steeped in reverent adoration, and you bowed your head with wonder and with praise, and said, "Great God! how infinite art Thou?" Have you never, in looking upon God's pure earth, when you have seen the mountains, and the clouds, and the rivers, and the floods, said:

> *These are your glorious works, Parent of good,*
> *Almighty! Thine this universal frame,*
> *Thus wondrous fair: Thyself how wondrous then?*

Oh! Methinks you must have had some glowing bursts of devotion. Yes, there have been moments when we could bow before God, when we felt our own nothingness and knew that He was all in all. Ah! If you can get such thoughts as these, my friends, this morning, I know that the next thought akin to this will be: "Let the whole earth be filled with His glory. Amen and Amen." You cannot bow before God and adore Him yourself without wishing that all the rest of mankind should do the same.

And the thought has gone further: you have wished that even inanimate objects might praise Him. Oh! You mountains, let the shaggy woods upon your crowns wave in adoration. Adore Him, adore Him, for He is worthy of all adoration; let Him ever be extolled. You cannot, I repeat, have great thoughts of God yourselves without spontaneously rising up and saying, "Let the whole earth be filled with His glory. Amen and Amen."

Turn your eyes yonder. What see you there? You see the Son of God stepping from the place of His glory, casting aside the garments of His majesty, and robing Himself in garments of clay. Do you see Him yonder? He is nailed to a cross. Can you behold Him as His head hangs meekly on His breast? Can you catch the accents of His lips when He says, "Father, forgive them"? Do you see Him with the thorn-crown still about His brow, with bleeding head, and hands, and feet? And does not your soul burst with adoration when you see Him giving Himself for your sins? Can you look upon this miracle of miracles, the death of the Son of God, without feeling reverence stirred within your bosom—a marvelous adoration that language never can express?

David's Dying Prayer

No, I am sure you cannot. You bow yourself before that cross, you close your eyes that are already filled with tears, and as you bend your head upon the mount of Calvary, I hear you say, "Jesus, have mercy upon me." And when you feel the blood applied to your conscience and know that He has blotted out your sins, you are not a man unless you start from your knees and cry, "Let the whole earth be filled with His glory. Amen and Amen."

Gaze a moment longer. The man that died for sinners sleeps within a grave. A little while He sleeps, until the angel rolls away the stone and gives Him liberty. Do you behold Him, as He wakes up from His slumber, and radiant with majesty and glorious with light, affrights His guard and stands a risen man? Do you see Him, as He climbs to heaven, as He ascends to the paradise of God, sitting at the right hand of His Father till His enemies are made His footstool? Do you see Him, as principalities and powers bow before Him, as cherubim and seraphim cast their crowns at His feet? Do you hear Him? Do you hear Him intercede, and do you hear also the music of the glorified spirits, ever chanting perpetual lays before His throne? And do you not wish that we might "Prepare new honors for His name, And songs before unknown"? It is impossible to see the glorified Christ with the eye of faith without exclaiming afterwards, "Let the whole earth be filled with His glory. Amen and Amen."

PURSUING THE OBJECT OF THIS PRAYER

First, you cannot pray this prayer unless you seek in your own life to remove every impediment to the spread of Christ's kingdom. How can the same lip that cursed God say, "Let the whole earth be filled with His glory. Amen and Amen." You cannot say it, sir, you who break His commandments and violate His laws and run riot against His government. Is there anything in our character and conduct that tends to prevent the spread of the gospel? There are many members of the churches everywhere whose characters are such that if they remain what they are, Christ's gospel never can fill the whole earth, for it cannot fill their hearts. We must look well to ourselves, by God's Spirit, or else we must not pray this prayer: "Let the whole earth be filled with His glory. Amen and Amen."

And there is my friend Mr. Save-All. I am sure he cannot pray this prayer. A contribution is requested to assist the cause in so doing. Oh! No, not at all. We want something in the ministry a little different before even ministers can pray this prayer in sincerity. I am not finding fault with any of my brethren, but I would recommend them to preach thirteen times a week, and then they can pray this prayer a little better. Three times a week would not do for me. It would hurt my constitution; preaching thirteen times a week is a good, healthy exercise. But you shut yourself up in your study, or what is ten times worse, you do nothing at all, but just take it easy all the week till the Sunday comes and then borrow a sermon out of an old magazine, or buy one of the helps for ministers, or take down one of Charles Simeon's skeletons and preach it. My good man, you cannot pray in that fashion. It cannot be, speaking after the manner of men, unless we each of us labor and endeavor, as God shall help us, to extend the kingdom of our Master.

And now, my friends, have I been urging you to an impossible toil? Have I been telling Christian men to pray for that which never can be granted? Ah! No, blessed be God, we are taught to pray for nothing but that which God has been pleased to give. He has told us to pray that His kingdom may come, and His kingdom will come, and come most assuredly, too.

Beloved, we will wait awhile. We will still continue on this side with our Master; for though we are fighters now, we shall be winners by and by. Yes, man, woman, you who are unknown, unnoted, but are striving for your Master, by prayer and praise and labor, the day is coming when every one of you shall have a crown of victory! The hour is coming when your heart shall beat high, for you shall share the conquest. We who have borne the brunt of the fight shall have a share of the glory; the victors shall divide the spoil, and we shall divide the spoil with them. You, tried, afflicted, forgotten and unknown, you shall soon have the palm branch in your hand, and you shall ride in triumph through the streets of earth and heaven, when your Master shall make show of principalities and powers openly in the day of His victory! Only continue, only wrestle on, and you shalt be crowned.

But I have one word to say, and then Amen. In Roman warfare there were special rewards given for special works. There was the mural crown for the man who first scaled the rampart and stood upon the wall. I am looking on this great congregation with a thought in my mind that agitates my spirit. Young men! Is there not one among you who can win a mural crown? Is there not one that can say in his heart, "Here am I, send me"? Are there no Pauls now? Have we none who will be apostles for the Lord of hosts? I think I see one who, putting his lips together, makes the silent resolve. O Lord, accept that young man! Your brother's heart beats with you; go, and go to victory. We will all pray this prayer in our houses alone: "Let the whole earth be filled with His glory. Amen and Amen." You who are enemies to God, beware, beware, beware! It will be a hard thing to be found on the side of the enemy in the great battle of right.

TITLE:
The Golden Key of Prayer

TEXT:
Jeremiah 33:3

SUMMARY:
Spurgeon divides this sermon into three sections. The first section shows that *prayer is commanded*. It is not a recommendation; it is commanded. There is secondly an *answer promised*. Spurgeon then highlights the *encouragement to faith in the prayer*. Spurgeon calls to mind that prayer is the best means of study. Many points of application are given for suffering, work, and for interceding for others.

NOTABLE QUOTES

"We are not merely counseled and recommended to pray, but we are bidden to pray."

"If God be true, you cannot seek mercy at His hands through Jesus Christ and get a negative reply."

A sermon preached by Charles H. Spurgeon on March 12, 1865. *Metropolitan Tabernacle Pulpit*, vol. 3.

4

The Golden Key of Prayer

"Call to Me, and I will answer you, and show you great and mighty things, which you do not know."

JEREMIAH 33:3

SOME OF THE MOST LEARNED WORKS in the world smell of the midnight oil, but the most spiritual and most comforting books and sayings of men usually have a savor about them of prison-damp. I might quote many instances: John Bunyan's *Pilgrim* may suffice instead of a hundred others; and this good text of ours, all moldy and chill with the prison in which Jeremiah lay, nevertheless has a brightness and a beauty about it, which it might never have had if it had not come as a cheering word to the prisoner of the Lord, shut up in the court of the prison-house. God's people have always in their worst condition found out the best of their God. He is good at all times, but He seems to be at His best when they are at their worst. They who dive in the sea of affliction bring up rare pearls. You whose bones have been ready to come through the skin through long lying upon the weary couch, you who have seen your earthly goods carried away from you and have been reduced well-nigh to penury, you who have gone to the grave yet seven times till you have feared that your last earthly friend would be borne away by unpitying Death, you have proved that He is a faithful God, and that as your tribulations abound, so your consolations also abound by Christ Jesus. My prayer is, in taking this text this morning, that some other prisoners of the Lord may have its joyous promise spoken home to them, that you who are shut up and cannot come forth by reason of present heaviness of spirit may hear Him say, as with a soft whisper in your ears and in your hearts, "Call to Me, and I will answer you, and show you great and mighty things, which you do not know."

PRAYER IS COMMANDED

We are not merely counseled and recommended to pray, but we are bidden to pray. This is great condescension. So strange is the infatuation of man on the one hand, which makes him need a command to be merciful to his own soul, and so marvelous is the condescension of our gracious God on the other hand, that He issues a command of love without which not a man of Adam would partake of the gospel feast.

In the matter of prayer it is even so. God's own people need, or else they would not receive it, a command to pray. How is this? Because, dear friends, we are very subject to fits of worldliness, if indeed that be not our usual state. We do not forget to eat; we do not forget to take the shop shutters down; we do not forget to be diligent in business; we do not forget to go to our beds to rest; but we often do forget to wrestle with God in prayer and to spend, as we ought to spend, long periods in consecrated fellowship with our Father and our God. With too many professors the ledger is so bulky that you cannot move it, and the Bible, representing their devotion, is so small that you might almost put it in your waistcoat pocket.

Hours for the world! Moments for Christ! The world has the best and our closet the parings of our time. We give our strength and freshness to the ways of mammon and our fatigue and languor to the ways of God. Hence we need to be commanded to attend to that very act which ought to be our greatest happiness, as it is our highest privilege to perform—to meet with our God.

He understands what heavy hearts we have sometimes, when under a sense of sin. Satan says to us, "Why should you pray? How can you hope to prevail? In vain you say, 'I will arise and go to my Father,' for you are not worthy to be one of His hired servants. How can you see the King's face after you have played the traitor against Him? How will you dare to approach unto the altar when you have yourself defiled it and when the sacrifice you would bring there is a poor, polluted one?"

O brethren, it is well for us that we are commanded to pray, or else in times of heaviness we might give it up. If God command me, unfit as I may be, I will creep to the footstool of grace. And since He says, "Pray without ceasing," though my words fail me and my heart itself will wander, yet I will stammer out the wishes of my hungering soul and say, "O God, at least teach me to pray and help me to prevail with You."

Are we not commanded to pray also because of our frequent unbelief? This is a case quite out of the list of those things wherein God hath interposed, and, therefore (says the devil), if you were in any other position, you might rest upon the mighty arm of God, but here your prayer will not avail you. Either it is too trivial a matter, or it is too connected with temporals, or else it is a matter in which you have sinned too much, or else it is too high, too hard, too complicated a piece of business that you have no right to take that before God! So suggests the foul fiend of hell. Therefore, there stands written as an everyday precept suitable to every case into which a Christian can be cast, "Call to Me."

We must not leave our first part till we have made another remark. We ought to be very glad that God hath given us this command in His Word that it may be sure and abiding. You may turn to fifty passages where the same precept is uttered. I do not often read in Scripture, "You shalt not kill," or, "You shalt not covet." Twice the law is given, but I often read gospel precepts, for if the law be given twice, the gospel is given seventy times seven. For every precept that I cannot keep, I find a thousand precepts that are sweet and pleasant for me to keep by reason of the power of the Holy Spirit that dwells in the children of God.

And this command to pray is insisted upon again and again. It may be a seasonable exercise for some of you to find out how often in Scripture you are told to pray. You will be surprised to find how many times such words as these are given. Come, Christian, you ought never to question whether you have a right to pray; you should never ask, "May I be permitted to come into His presence?" When you have so many commands (and God's commands are all promises and all enablings), you may come boldly unto the throne of heavenly grace by the new and living way through the torn veil.

But there are times when God not only commands His people to pray in the Bible, but He also commands them to pray directly by the monitions of His Holy Spirit. You who know the inner life comprehend me at once. You feel on a sudden, possibly in the midst of business, the pressing thought that you must retire to pray. You may not at first take particular notice of the inclination, but it comes again and again and again: "Retire and pray!"

I find that in the matter of prayer, I am myself very much like a water wheel that runs well when there is plenty of water, but that turns with very little force when the brook is growing shallow. Now, it strikes me that whenever our Lord gives you the special inclination to pray, that you should double your diligence. You ought always to pray and not to faint, yet when He gives you the special longing after prayer, and you feel a peculiar aptness and enjoyment in it, you have, over and above the command that is constantly binding, another command that should compel you to cheerful obedience.

At such times, I think we may stand in the position of David, to whom the Lord said, "when you hear the sound of marching in the tops of the mulberry trees, then you shall advance quickly" (2 Sam. 5:24). That going in the tops of the mulberry trees may have been the footfalls of angels hastening to the help of David, and then David was to smite the Philistines, and when God's mercies are coming, their footfalls are our desires to pray, and our desires to pray should be at once an indication that the set time to favor Zion is come.

Sow plentifully now, for you can sow in hope; plough joyously now, for your harvest is sure. Wrestle now, Jacob, for you are about to be made a prevailing prince, and your name shall be called Israel. Now is your time, spiritual merchantmen; the market is high, trade much; your profit shall be large. See to it that you use right well the golden hour and reap your harvest while the sun shines. When we enjoy visitations from on high, we should be peculiarly constant in prayer; and if some other duty less pressing should have the go-by for a season, it will not be amiss, and we shall be no loser. For when God bids us specially pray by the monitions of His Spirit, then should we bestir ourselves in prayer.

AN ANSWER PROMISED

We ought not to tolerate for a minute the ghastly and grievous thought that God will not answer prayer. His nature, as manifested in Christ Jesus, demands it. He has revealed Himself in the gospel as a God of love, full of grace and truth. How can He refuse to help those of His creatures who humbly in His own appointed way seek His face and favor?

Let us recollect next His past character as well as His nature.

I mean the character that He has won for Himself by His past deeds of grace. Consider, my brethren, that one stupendous display of bounty—if I were to mention a thousand, I could not give a better illustration of the character of God than that one deed—"He who did not spare His own Son, but delivered Him up for us all, how shall He not with Him also freely give us all things?" (Rom. 8:32). If the Lord did not refuse to listen to my voice when I was a guilty sinner and an enemy, how can He disregard my cry now that I am justified and saved? How is it that He heard the voice of my misery when my heart knew it not, and would not seek relief, if after all He will not hear me now that I am His child, His friend? The streaming wounds of Jesus are the sure guarantees for answered prayer.

You misread Calvary if you think that prayer is useless. But, beloved, we have the Lord's own promise for it, and He is a God who cannot lie. "Call upon Me in the day of trouble; I will deliver you" (Ps. 50:15). Has He not said, "whatever things you ask when you pray, believe that you receive them, and you will have them" (Mark 11:24)? We cannot pray, indeed, unless we believe this doctrine. And if we have any question at all about whether our prayer will be heard, we are comparable to him who wavers: "he who doubts is like a wave of the sea driven and tossed by the wind. For let not that man suppose that he will receive anything from the Lord" (James 1:6–7).

Furthermore, our own experience leads us to believe that God will answer prayer. I must not speak for you, but I may speak for myself. If there be anything I know, anything that I am quite assured of beyond all question, it is that praying breath is never spent in vain. If no other man here can say it, I dare to say it, and I know that I can prove it. My own conversion is the result of prayer, long, affectionate, earnest, importunate. Parents prayed for me; God heard their cries, and here I am to preach the gospel.

Since then I have adventured upon some things that were far beyond my capacity as I thought; but I have never failed, because I have cast myself upon the Lord. You know as a church that I have not scrupled to indulge large ideas of what we might do for God, and we have accomplished all that we purposed. I have sought God's aid in all my manifold undertakings, and though I cannot tell here the story of my private life in God's work, if it were written it would be a standing proof that there is a God that answers prayer. He has heard my prayers, not now and then, nor once nor twice, but so many times, that it has grown into a habit with me to spread my case before God with the absolute certainty that whatsoever I ask of God, He will give to me. It is not now a "perhaps" or a possibility. I know that my Lord answers me, and I dare not doubt; it was indeed folly if I did.

In all labor there is profit, but most of all in the work of intercession. I am sure of this, for I have reaped it. As I put trust in the queen's money and have never failed yet to buy what I want when I produce the cash, so I put trust in God's promises and mean to do so till I find that He shall once tell me that they are base coin and will not do to trade within heaven's market.

Remember that prayer is always to be offered in submission to God's will, that when we say God hears prayer, we do not intend by that that He always gives us literally what we ask for.

We do mean, however, that He gives us what is best for us. And if He does not give us the mercy we ask for in silver, He bestows it upon us in gold. If He does not take away the thorn in the flesh, yet He says, "My grace is sufficient for you," that comes to the same in the end. We never offer up prayer without inserting that clause, either in spirit or in words, "nevertheless not My will, but Yours, be done" (Luke 22:42). We can only pray without an "if" when we are quite sure that our will must be God's will because God's will is fully our will.

ENCOURAGEMENT TO FAITH

Let us just remark that this was originally spoken to a prophet in prison; therefore, it applies in the first place to every teacher, and indeed, as every teacher must be a learner, it has a bearing upon every learner in divine truth. The best way by which a prophet and teacher and learner can know the reserved truths, the higher and more mysterious truths of God, is by waiting upon God in prayer.

I noticed very specially yesterday in reading the book of Daniel, how Daniel found out Nebuchadnezzar's dream. The soothsayers, the magicians, the astrologers of the Chaldees all failed. What did Daniel do? He set himself to prayer, and knowing that the prayer of a united body of men has more prevalence than the prayer of one, we find that Daniel called together his brethren and bade them unite with him in earnest prayer that God would be pleased of His infinite mercy to open up the vision.

And in the case of John, you remember, he saw a book in the right hand of Him who sat on the throne—a book sealed with seven seals that no one was worthy to open. What did John do? He wept much, and John's tears were his liquid prayers, the sacred keys by which the folded book was opened.

Brethren in the ministry, I pray you remember that prayer is your best means of study. Like Daniel, you shall understand the dream and its interpretation when you have sought God. And like John, you will see the seven seals of precious truth unloosed after you have wept much. Stones are not broken except by an earnest use of the hammer, and the stonebreaker usually goes down on his knees. Use the hammer of diligence, and let the knee of prayer be exercised, too. As Luther said, "To have prayed well is to have studied well."

We must not, however, stop there. We have applied the text to only one case; it is applicable to a hundred. The saint may expect to discover deeper experience and to know more of the higher life and scriptural life by being much in prayer. There are different translations of my text. One version renders it, "I will shew you great and fortified things which you knowest not." Another reads it, "Great and reserved things which you knowest not."

Now, all the developments of spiritual life are not alike easy of attainment. My brethren, there are heights in experimental knowledge of the things of God that the eagle's eye of acumen and philosophic thought has never seen, and there are secret paths that the lion's whelp of reason and judgment has not learned to travel. God alone can bear us there, but the chariot in which He takes us up, and the fiery steeds with which that chariot is dragged, are prevailing prayers. Prevailing prayer is victorious over the God of mercy. Prevailing prayer takes the Christian to Carmel and enables him to cover heaven with clouds of blessing and earth with floods of mercy. Prevailing prayer bears the Christian aloft to Pisgah and shows him the inheritance reserved, and it elevates him to Tabor and transfigures him, till in the likeness of his Lord, as He is, so are we also in this world. If you would reach to something higher than ordinary groveling experience, look to the Rock that is higher than you, and look with the eye of faith through the windows of importunate prayer. To grow in experience then, there must be much prayer.

You must have patience with me while I apply this text to two or three more cases. It is certainly true of the sufferer under trial: if he waits upon God in prayer much, he shall receive greater deliverances than he has ever dreamed of. So often it will happen that God will not only help His people through the miry places of the way, so that they may just stand on the other side of the slough, but He will bring them safely far on the journey.

That was a remarkable miracle, when in the midst of the storm Jesus Christ came walking upon the sea, the disciples received Him into the ship, and not only was the sea calm, but it is recorded, "immediately the boat was at the land where they were going" (John 6:21). That was a mercy over and above what they asked. Let us then, dear friends, when we are in great trial only say, "Now I am in prison; like Jeremiah I will pray as he did, for I have God's command to do it. And I will look out as he did, expecting that He will show me reserved mercies which I know nothing of at present." He will not merely bring His people through the battle, covering their heads in it, but He will bring them forth with banners waving, to divide the spoil with the mighty, and to claim their portion with the strong. Expect great things of a God who gives such great promises as these.

Again, here is encouragement for the worker. Most of you are doing something for Christ. I am happy to be able to say this, knowing that I do not flatter you. My dear friends, wait upon God much in prayer, and you have the promise that He will do greater things for you than you know of. We know not how much capacity for usefulness there may be in us. When Christ by His Spirit grips you, what can you not do? Truly you may adopt Paul's language and say, "I can do all things through Christ who strengthens me" (Phil. 4:13).

I shall not detain you many minutes longer, but I want to notice that this promise ought to prove useful for comforting those who intercede for others. You who are calling upon God to save your children, to bless your neighbors, to remember your husbands or your wives in mercy, may take comfort from today's text. You cannot guess how greatly God will bless you. Only go and stand at His door. If you do not beg at all, you will get nothing; but if you beg, He may not only give you, as it were, the bones and broken meat, but He may say to the servant at His table, "Take you that dainty meat, and set that before the poor man."

Ruth went to glean; she expected to get a few good ears. but Boaz said, "Let her glean even among the sheaves, and do not reproach her." She found a husband where she only expected to find a handful of barley. So in prayer for others, God may give us such mercies that we shall be astounded at them, since we expected but little.

Now, this word to close with. Some of you seek your own conversion. God has quickened you to solemn prayer about your own souls. You are not content to go to hell; you want heaven. You want washing in the precious blood. You want eternal life. Dear friends, I pray you take this text; God Himself speaks it to you: "Call to Me, and I will answer you, and show you great and mighty things, which you do not know." At once take God at His word. Get home, go into your chamber and shut the door, and try Him. If God be true, you cannot seek mercy at His hands through Jesus Christ and get a negative reply. He must, for His own promise and character bind Him to it, open mercy's gate to you who knock with all your heart. God help you, believing in Christ Jesus, to cry aloud unto God, and His answer of peace is already on the way to meet you. You shall hear Him say, "Your sins which are many are all forgiven."

TITLE:
Prayer, the Proof of Godliness

TEXT:
Psalm 32:6

SUMMARY:
Spurgeon wants to show the mark of the godly man, namely prayer. He begins first by saying prayer is the universal mark of godliness. It is the mark of godliness not only in infancy but throughout life. There is also a potent motive for praying. One of those is because God heard the prayers of such a great sinner like David. We all need pardon daily. Spurgeon lastly wants to highlight the occasion when prayer is most useful. He highlights various times and circumstances in our time on earth where it is especially needed.

NOTABLE QUOTES

"Prayer is the mark of godliness in its infancy."

"The man who has most grace will pray most."

"So long as you live here and pray to God, He has promised to answer. Though it be the eleventh hour, do not hesitate to pray."

A sermon preached by Charles H. Spurgeon on October 27, 1887. *Metropolitan Tabernacle Pulpit*, vol. 41.

5

Prayer, the Proof of Godliness

For this cause everyone who is godly shall pray to You in a time when You may be found.

PSALM 32:6

ALL MEN ARE NOT GODLY. Alas! The ungodly are the great majority of the human race. And all men who are to some extent godly are not equally godly. The man who fears God and desires truly to know Him has some measure of godliness. The man who has begun to trust the Savior whom God has set forth as the great propitiation for sin has a blessed measure of godliness. The man whose communion with God is constant, whose earnest prayers and penitential tears are often observed of the great Father and who sighs after fuller and deeper acquaintance with the Lord—this man is godly in a still higher sense. And he who, by continual fellowship with God, has become like Him, upon whom the image of Christ has been photographed, he is the godly man. The man who finds his God everywhere, who sees Him in the works of His hands, the man who traces everything to God, the man who looks to God for everything, takes every suit to the throne of grace, and every petition to the mercy seat, the man who could not live without his God, to whom God is his exceeding joy, the help and the health of his countenance, the man who dwells in God—this is the godly man. This is the man who shall dwell forever with God.

Judge by these test, whether you are godly or not. The text itself is a test by which we may tell whether we are among the godly: "For this cause everyone who is godly shall pray to You in a time when You may be found." In these words we have, first, the universal mark of godly men: they pray unto God. Then we have, secondly, a potent motive for praying. And then, thirdly, we have the special occasion when prayer is most useful: when God may be found.

THE UNIVERSAL MARK OF GODLINESS

When a man is beginning to be godly, this is the first sign of the change that is being wrought in him. Prayer is the mark of godliness in its infancy. Until he has come to pleading and petitioning, we cannot be sure that the divine life is in him at all. There may be desires, but if they never turn to prayers, we may fear that they are as the morning cloud, which soon passes away. There may be some signs of holy thought about the man, but if that thought never deepens into prayer, we may be afraid that the thought will be like the seed sown upon the hard highway. But when the man comes to real pleading terms with God, you begin to hope that now he is indeed a godly man. Prayer is the breath of life in the newborn believer. Prayer is the first cry by which it is known that the newborn child truly lives. If he does not pray, you may suspect that he has only a name to live and that he lacks spiritual life.

Prayer is equally the mark of godliness in all stages of its growth. The man who has most grace will pray most. Take my word for it as certain, that when you and I have most grace, there is more of prayer and praise in us than there was before. If you pray less than you once did, then judge yourself to be less devout, to be less in fellowship with God, to be, in fact, less godly. I know of no better thermometer to your spiritual temperature than this, the measure of the intensity of your prayer.

I am not speaking about the quantity of prayer, for there are some who make long prayers as a pretense. But I am speaking about the reality of it, the intensity of it. Prayer is best measured by weight rather than by length and breadth, and in proportion as you grow in grace, you will grow in prayerfulness. When the child of God reaches the measure of the fullness of the stature of a man in Christ Jesus, then he becomes like Elias, a man mighty in prayer. One such man in a church may save it from ruin. One such man in a nation may bring down upon it untold blessings. He is the godliest man who has most power with God in his secret pleadings, and he who has most power with God in his secret pleadings has it because he abounds in godliness.

Every one that is godly shall pray unto the Lord, whether he be but the babe in grace who lisps his few broken sentences or the strong man in Christ who lays hold upon the covenant angel with Jacob's mighty resolve. The prayers may vary as the degree of godliness differs, but every godly man has, from the beginning to the end of his spiritual life, this distinguishing mark, "Behold, he prays."

Further, dear friends, true prayer is an infallible mark of godliness. If you do not pray, remember that "a prayerless soul is a Christless soul." You know how often it has been the case that the highest professions of holiness have been sometimes accompanied by the practice of the deadliest vices. For instance, wherever the doctrine of human perfection has been much held, it has almost always engendered some horrible licentiousness, some desperate filthiness of the flesh. In like manner, I have known persons to become, as they say, so conformed to the mind of God, so perfectly in accord with the divine will, that they have not felt it necessary to pray. This is the devil in white, and the devil in white is more of a devil than when he is dressed in black. If anything leads you to decline in prayerfulness, or to abstain altogether from prayer, it is an evil thing, disguise it as you may.

But wherever there is real prayer in the soul, take it as certain that the lingering of holy desire in the spirit proves that there is life in the spirit still. If the Lord enables you to pray, I beseech you, do not despair. If you have to pray with many a groan, and sigh, and tear, think none the less of your prayers for that reason. I have known what it is to come away from the throne of grace feeling that I have not prayed at all. I have despised my prayer and wept over it; yet, in looking back, I have thought, "I wish I could pray as I did in the time when I thought that I did not pray at all." We are usually poor judges of our own prayers. If you pray a truly spiritual prayer, this shall be indeed a sure mark that the Spirit of God is striving within you and that you are already a child of God.

Once more, beloved friends, prayer is natural to the godly man. I do think that it is a good thing to have set times for prayer, but I am sure that it would be a dreadful thing to confine prayer to any time or season, for to the godly man, prayer comes to be like breathing, like sighing, like crying. Jacob could not always go and spend a night in prayer; possibly he never spent another whole night in prayer in all his life after that memorable one. But when he spent that one by the brook Jabbok, he could "do no other," as Luther said. You want the prayer that rises from you freely, like the fountain that leaped from the smitten rock. Prayer should be the natural outflow of the soul; you should pray because you must pray, not because the set time for praying has arrived, but because your heart must cry unto your Lord.

A prayerless condition should be a miserable and unhappy condition to a child of God, and he should have no rest until he finds that once more his spirit can truly pour itself out before the living God. When you are in a right state of heart, praying is as simple as breathing. That is how godly men come to be at last; it gets to be as natural to them to pray as to breathe. You do not notice all day long how many times you breathe; when you come home at night, you do not say, "I have breathed so many times today." No, of course you do not notice your breathing unless you happen to be asthmatical, and when a man gets asthmatical in prayer, he begins to notice his praying, but he who is in good sound spiritual health breathes freely, like a living soul before the living God, and his life becomes one continual season of prayer.

To such a man, prayer is a happy and consoling exercise. It is no task, no effort. His prayer, when he is truly godly and living near to God, is an intense delight. When he can get away from business for a few quiet minutes of communion with God, when he can steal away from the noise of the world and get a little time alone, these are the joys of his life. These are the delights that help us to wait with patience through the long days of our exile till the King shall come and take us home to dwell with Himself forever.

Those prayers of the godly, however, may be presented in a great many forms. Some praying takes the good form of action, and an act may be a prayer. To love our fellowmen and to desire their good is a kind of consolidated practical prayer. There comes to be a prayer to God in giving alms, or in preaching the gospel, or in trying to win a wanderer, or in taking a child upon your knee, and talking to it about the Savior. Such acts are often most acceptable prayers, but when you cannot act thus, it is well to pour out your heart before the Lord in words. And when you cannot do that, it is sweet to sit quite still and look up to Him, and even as the lilies pour out their fragrance before Him who made them, so do you, even without speaking, worship God in that deep adoration which is too eloquent for language, that holy nearness that, because it is so near, dares not utter a sound lest it should break the spell of the divine silence that engirds it. Frost of the mouth, but flow of the soul, is often a

A POTENT MOTIVE FOR PRAYER

The motive seems to be, first, because God heard such a great sinner as David was. Let us learn from it this lesson that God has heard the prayer of a great sinner. There may be, in this house of prayer, someone who has gone into gross and grievous sin, and this reading of the passage may be a message from the Lord to that person.

David had sinned very foully, and he had added deceit to his sin. His evil deeds have made the ungodly rail at godliness even until the present day, so that infidels ask in contempt, "Is this the man after God's own heart?" It was an awful sin that he committed, but there came to him a time of finding out his sin. His heart was broken in penitence, and then he went to God and found mercy. He said, in effect, that it was so wonderful that such a wretch as he was should be forgiven, that every godly man, as long as the world stood, would believe in the confession of sin to the Lord and in the power of prayer to obtain pardon for the guilty.

It is sometimes necessary to us, when we are under a sense of sin, to think of such sinners as Manasseh, Magdalene, the dying thief, Saul of Tarsus. There are times, even with those whom God has greatly blessed, when nothing but the sinner's Savior will do for them and when they feel that, if there were not salvation for the vilest of the vile, there would be no salvation for them. So God gives us a case like David, so that everyone who is godly may pray unto him in the time of finding out his sin.

Another motive for prayer the text brings before us is that we all need pardon daily. I hope that all of you pray unto God daily for the forgiveness of sins. I am sure that all the godly among you do so. If you commit no sins, then the Savior made a great mistake when He left us the prayer, "Forgive us our trespasses." What is the need of that petition if we have no trespasses to be forgiven? But for this, that is, for the pardon of his sin, everyone who is godly will pray unto the Lord.

And every one who is godly will pray unto God because he has received the pardon of sin. You remember when you made your confession to the Judge of all and received absolution from Him. You recollect when, with broken heart and downcast eye, you acknowledged your sin unto Him, and He put away your transgression. Well then, that is the reason why you should always be praying. He who heard you then will still hear you. He who put away your sin then will continue to put away your sin by that foot-washing that He gives to us continually. Blessed be God, we shall not cease to pray for pardon although we have received pardon; we will crave the daily renewal of the divine token of reconciliation. If we received it when we were sinners, much more shall we receive it now that we are reconciled to God by the death of His Son. If we received it when we were outcasts, much more shall we receive it now that we are His dear children.

Again, "For this cause everyone who is godly shall pray to You," that is to say, because troubles come, for the connection teaches us this lesson. Brethren, the Lord takes care to keep us praying, does He not, by giving us constant needs? Suppose that I had a friend upon whom I was dependent, and whose society I greatly loved, and that he said to me, "I will give you, in a lump sum, as much money as will last you till this time next year, and then you can come and see me, and receive another year's portion; or, as you like to come to my house, would you prefer to have the amount quarterly?"

I should reply, "I will choose the latter plan, for then I should come to you four times in the year and have four dinners with you."

"Well, then, would you like it monthly?"

"Oh, yes! I would like to come monthly and spend a day with you every month."

"Perhaps," says he, "you would like to come daily."

"Oh, yes! I should prefer that; I should like to have a daily portion at your table."

"Perhaps you would like to stop with me always. Perhaps you would like to receive everything from my own hand and have nothing but what I give you."

"Oh! Yes, my friend, this continual indebtedness, this constant dependence, would give me so many opportunities of better knowing you whom I love so much that I should like to have it so."

You who like may go and gather a week's manna; it will stink before the end of the week. I like to have mine fresh every day, just as it comes warm from the ovens of heaven and ready for the heavenly appetite of the man who learns to live upon the daily gift of God. For this shall everyone who is godly pray unto God. He shall have trouble to drive him; he shall have grace to draw him; he shall have weights to lift him; and they shall be so adjusted that, though they threaten to hold him down, they shall really raise him up.

Once more, I think that, broadly speaking, the word *this* here means, "Because God does hear prayer, everyone who is godly shall pray to you." Now, dear friends, it always will be a dispute between the true believer and the mere professor whether God hears prayer. Of course, the outside world will always sneer at the idea of God hearing prayer. When I stand here and declare solemnly that hundreds and even thousands of times God has answered my prayers, I claim to be as much accepted as an honest witness as I should be in the High Court of Justice, and I can bring forward not myself only, but scores and hundreds of you.

When anyone says, "God does not hear prayer," I am sorry for the poor soul that dares to make an assertion about a thing he has never tested and tried. God does hear prayer, and because He hears it, we will call upon Him as long as we live. "For this cause everyone who is godly shall pray to You in a time when You may be found." Prayer does move the arm that moves the world, though nothing is put out of gear by our praying. The God who ordained the effects that are to follow prayer ordained the prayer itself; it is a part of the grand machinery by which the world swings upon its hinges.

WHEN PRAYER IS MOST USEFUL

Is there any set time when God is to be found? Well, in general, it is the time of this mortal life. So long as you live here and pray

Prayer, the Proof of Godliness

to God, He has promised to answer. Though it be the eleventh hour, do not hesitate to pray. Christ's word is, "He who seeks finds" (Matt. 7:8). There is a special promise to those who seek the Lord early, but this does not exclude those who seek Him late. If you truly seek Him, He will be found by you.

I think, too, that the time of finding is under this gospel dispensation. God has always heard prayer, but there seems to be a larger liberty allowed us in prayer now. The mercy seat is unveiled, and the veil is rent away that we may come with boldness.

But besides that, there are special times of finding God, namely, in visitations of His Spirit. Revival times are grand times for prayer. How many there are who put in their suit with God because they feel moved thereto by a heavenly impulse!

In closing, I will dwell only upon this one point: there are special times of finding for individuals, and one of these is the time of the finding out of sin. The time when you will find out sin is the time when you will find God. "Why!" say you, "it is a horrible thing for me to find out my sin." It is, in itself; but it is the best time to find out God. When your eyes are blinded with tears of penitence, you can best see the Savior. Do not say, "I find myself to be so guilty, and therefore I have no hope." Nay, rather, because you find yourself to be guilty, therefore have hope, for the Savior came to seek and to save such guilty ones as you are. The time, I say, when sin finds us out, and we are humbled and ashamed, is the time when we may find our God through Jesus Christ.

So, too, a time of decision is a time for finding God. Some have not decided whether they will live for the world and perish or seek Christ and live eternally. But when the Spirit of God comes upon you and you say to yourself, "I must find Jesus Christ, I must get forgiveness, and lay hold of eternal life; give me Christ, or else I die," you shall have Him. God has promised that, if we seek Him with our whole heart, He will be found of us. When you are decided for God thoroughly and intensely, it will be with you a time of finding.

So will it be when you come to God in full submission. Some of you have not laid down your weapons of rebellion yet. You cannot be reconciled to God while your sword is in your hand; down with it, man! Some of you have fine feathers on your helmets, and you come before God as great captains; off with those feathers! He will accept you in rags, but not in ribbons. He will receive you if you come confessing your sin, but not boasting of your supposed merits. Down with you into the very dust. Yield to God. Oh, that His mercy might make us all pliant as the willow before His mighty power! Then shall we find peace through Christ.

When the whole soul is bent on seeking Christ, then will the Lord speedily appear, and it shall be a time of finding. But especially is it a time of finding when the heart at last trusts wholly and implicitly to the Lamb of God that takes away the sin of the world. You shall find that God has found you when you have done with yourself and taken the blood and righteousness of Christ to be the sole hope of your soul. God lead you to this, dear hearers, this very hour!

TITLE:
Lead Us Not into Temptation

TEXT:
Matthew 6:13

SUMMARY:
Spurgeon first asks what suggests a prayer like this. His reason is watchfulness. He moves on from there to suggest that a horror of falling into sin again motivates this prayer, followed by a diffidence of human power. Spurgeon then asks what the temptations are that the prayer deprecates. He offers various suggestions, like the withdrawal of divine grace, providential conditions, and temptations of money and physical conditions. Spurgeon concludes with lessons this prayer teaches. We should never desire trial or temptation.

NOTABLE QUOTES

"Our heavenly Father has never meant to cuddle us up and keep us out of temptation, for that is no part of the system which He has wisely arranged for our education."

"Do nothing, my dear brother, of which you have need to be ashamed or that you would not wish others to copy."

A sermon preached by Charles H. Spurgeon in 1878. *Metropolitan Tabernacle Pulpit*, vol. 24.

6

Lead Us Not into Temptation

Lead us not into temptation.
MATTHEW 6:13 KJV

LOOKING OVER A BOOK OF ADDRESSES to young people the other day, I met with the outline of a discourse that struck me as being a perfect gem. The text is the Lord's Prayer, and the exposition is divided into most instructive heads. "Our Father which art in heaven": a child away from home. "Hallowed be your name": a worshiper. "Thy kingdom come": a subject. "Thy will be done in earth as it is in heaven": a servant. "Give us this day our daily bread": a beggar. "And forgive us our debts as we forgive our debtors": a sinner. "And lead us not into temptation but deliver us from evil": a sinner in danger of being a greater sinner still.

The titles are in every case most appropriate, and truthfully, they condense the petition. You will notice that the prayer is like a ladder. The petitions begin at the top and go downward. The first is a child of the heavenly Father—the highest possible position of man. It is a very high, gracious, exalted position, which by faith we dare to occupy when we intelligently say, "Our Father which art in heaven."

It is a step down to the next: "Hallowed be your name." Here we have a worshiper adoring with lowly reverence the thrice-holy God. A worshiper's place is a high one, but it attains not to the excellence of the child's position. Angels come as high as being worshipers, "Our Father." They must be content to be within one step of the highest, but they cannot reach the summit, for neither by adoption, regeneration, nor by union to Christ are they the children of God. "Abba, Father" is for men, not for angels, and therefore the worshiping sentence of the prayer is one step lower than the opening "Our Father."

The next petition is for us as subjects: "Thy kingdom come." The subject comes lower than the worshiper, for worship is an elevated engagement wherein man exercises a priesthood and is seen in lowly but honorable estate. The child worships and then confesses the great Father's royalty.

Descending still, the next position is that of a servant, "Thy will be done in earth as it is in heaven." That is another step lower than a subject, for her majesty the Queen has many subjects who are not her servants. The servant is a grade below the subject.

Everyone will own that the next petition is lower by far, for it is that of a beggar who has continually to appeal to charity, even for his livelihood: "Give us this day our daily bread." This is a fit place for us to occupy, who owe our all to the charity of heaven.

But there is a step lower than the beggar's, and that is the sinner's place. "Forgive" is lowlier than "give." "Forgive us our debts as we forgive our debtors." Here too we may each one take up his position, for no word better befits our unworthy lips than the prayer "Forgive." As long as we live and sin, we ought to weep and cry, "Have mercy on us, O Lord." And now, at the very bottom of the ladder, stands a sinner, afraid of yet greater sin, in extreme danger and in conscious weakness, sensible of past sin and fearful of it for the future; hear him as with trembling lip he cries in the words of our text, "Lead us not into temptation, but deliver us from evil."

And yet, dear friends, though I have thus described the prayer as a going downward, downward is in matters of grace much the same as upward, as we could readily show if time permitted. At any rate, the down-going process of the prayer might equally well illustrate the advance of the divine life in the soul. The last clause of the prayer contains in it a deeper inward experience than the earlier part of it.

Every believer is a child of God, a worshiper, a subject, a servant, a beggar, and a sinner, but it is not every man who perceives the allurements which beset him or his own tendency to yield to them. It is not every child of God, even when advanced in years, who knows to the full the meaning of being led into temptation, for some follow an easy path and are seldom buffeted, and others are such tender babes that they hardly know their own corruptions. Fully to understand our text a man should have had sharp brushes in the wars and have done battle against the enemy within his soul for many a day. He who has escaped as by the skin of his teeth offers this prayer with an emphasis of meaning. The man who has felt the fowler's net about him—the man who has been seized by the adversary and almost destroyed—he prays with awful eagerness, "Lead us not into temptation."

THE SPIRIT THAT PRAYS SUCH A PRAYER

What suggests such a prayer as this? First, from the position of the clause, I gather that it is suggested by watchfulness. This petition follows after the sentence, "Forgive us our debts." I will suppose the petition to have been answered, and the man's sin is forgiven.

What then? If you will look back upon your own lives, you will soon perceive what generally happens to a pardoned man, for "As in water face reflects face, so a man's heart reveals the man." One believing man's inner experience is like another's, and your own feelings were the same as mine. Very speedily after the penitent has received forgiveness and has the sense of it in his soul, he is tempted of the devil, for Satan cannot bear to lose his subjects. To meet this special assault, the Lord makes the heart watchful.

Perceiving the ferocity and subtlety of Satan's temptations, the newborn believer, rejoicing in the perfect pardon he has received, cries to God, "Lead us not into temptation." It is the fear of losing the joy of pardoned sin which thus cries out to the good Lord. It is a prayer of watchfulness, and mark you, though we have spoken of watchfulness as necessary at the commencement of the Christian life, it is equally needful even to the close. There is no hour in which a believer can afford to slumber. Watch, I pray you, when you are alone, for temptation, like a creeping assassin, has its dagger for solitary hearts. You must bolt and bar the door well if you would keep out the devil. Watch yourself in public, for temptations in troops cause their arrows to fly by day. The choicest companions you can select will not be without some evil influence upon you unless you be on your guard.

Next, it seems to me to be the natural prayer of holy horror at the very thought of falling again into sin. It would better for us to die at once than to live on and return to our first estate and bring dishonor upon the name of Jesus Christ our Lord. The prayer before us springs from the shrinking of the soul at the first approach of the tempter. The footfall of the fiend falls on the startled ear of the timid penitent; he quivers like an aspen leaf and cries out, "What, is he coming again? And is it possible that I may fall again? And may I once more defile these garments with that loathsome, murderous sin that slew my Lord? Keep me from so dire an evil. Lead me, I pray you, where you will, even through death's dark valley, but do not lead me into temptation, lest I fall and dishonor you." He who has once been caught in the steel trap carries the scars in his flesh and is horribly afraid of being again held by its cruel teeth.

The third feeling is also apparent: diffidence of personal strength. The man who feels himself strong enough for anything invites the battle that will prove his power. He is ready to be led into conflict. Not so the man who has been taught of God and has learned his own weakness; he does not want to be tried but seeks quiet places where he may be out of harm's way. Let him be tempted, and you will see how steadfast he will be, but he does not ask for conflict. Surely it is only those who have never smelled gunpowder or seen the corpses heaped in bloody masses on each other, that are so eager for the shot and shell, but your veteran would rather enjoy the piping times of peace.

No experienced believer ever desires spiritual conflict, though perchance some raw recruits may challenge it. In the Christian, a recollection of his previous weakness—his resolutions broken, his promises unkept—makes him pray that he may not in future be severely tested. He does not dare to trust himself again. He wants no fight with Satan or with the world, but he asks that if possible he may be kept from those severe encounters, and his prayer is, "Lead us not into temptation."

The wise believer shows a sacred diffidence, nay, I think I may say an utter despair of himself. Even though he knows that the power of God is strong enough for anything, yet is the sense of his weakness so heavy upon him that he begs to be spared too much trial. Hence the cry, "Lead us not into temptation."

Nor have I quite exhausted, I think, the phases of the spirit that suggest this prayer, for it seems to me to arise somewhat out of charity. "Charity?" say you. "How so?" Well, the connection is always to be observed, and by reading the preceding sentence in connection with it, we get the words, "as we forgive our debtors, and lead us not into temptation." We should not be too severe with those persons who have done wrong and offended us, but instead we pray, "Lord, lead us not into temptation."

It is true it was very wrong in that young man to deal so dishonestly with your goods. Still, you know, he was under great pressure from a strong hand and only yielded from compulsion. Do not be too severe. Do not say, "I will push the matter through; I will have the law of him." No, but wait awhile; let pity speak; let mercy's silver voice plead with you. Remember yourself lest you also be tempted, and pray, "Lead us not into temptation."

I am afraid that, badly as some behave under temptation, others of us might have done worse if we had been there. I like, if I can, to form a kind judgment of the erring, and it helps me to do so when I imagine myself to have been subject to their trials and to have looked at things from their point of view and to have been in their circumstances, and to have nothing of the grace of God to help me. Should I not have fallen as badly as they have done, or even gone beyond them in evil?

May not the day come to you who show no mercy in which you may have to ask mercy for yourselves? Did I say—may it not come to you? Nay, it must come to you. When leaving all below, you will have to take a retrospective view of your life and see much to mourn over, to what can you appeal then but to the mercy of God? And what if He should answer you, "An appeal was made to your mercy, and you had none. As you rendered unto others so will I render unto you." What answer would you have if God were so to treat you? Would not such an answer be just and right? Should not every man be paid in his own coin when he stands at the judgment seat? So I think that this prayer, "Lead us not into temptation," should often spring up from the heart through a charitable feeling toward others who have erred, who are of the same flesh and blood as ourselves.

Now, whenever you see the drunkard reel through the streets, do not glory over him but say, "Lead us not into temptation." When you take down the papers and read that men of position have betrayed their trust for gold, condemn their conduct if you will, but do not exult in your own steadfastness. Rather, cry in all humility, "Lead us not into temptation." When the poor girl seduced from the paths of virtue comes across your way, look not on her with the scorn that would give her up to destruction, but say, "Lead us not into temptation." It would teach us milder and gentler ways with sinful men and women if this prayer were as often in our hearts as it is upon our lips.

Once more, do you not think that this prayer breathes the spirit of confidence, confidence in God? There is a degree of tender familiarity and sacred boldness in this expression. Of course, God will lead me now that I am His child. Moreover, now that He has forgiven me, I know that He will not lead me where I can come to any harm. This my faith ought to know and believe, and yet for several reasons, there rises to my mind a fear lest His providence should conduct me where I shall be tempted. Is that fear right or wrong? It burdens my mind; may I go with it to my God? May I express in prayer this misgiving of soul? May I pour out this anxiety before the great, wise, loving God? Will it not be impertinent?

No, it will not, for Jesus puts the words into my mouth and says, "After this manner pray ye." You are afraid that He may lead you into temptation, but He will not do so. Or should He see fit to try you, He will also afford you strength to hold out to the end. He will be pleased in His infinite mercy to preserve you. Where He leads, it will be perfectly safe for you to follow, for His presence will make the deadliest air to become healthful. But since instinctively you have a dread lest you should be conducted where the fight will be too stern and the way too rough, tell it to your heavenly Father without reserve.

You know at home if a child has any little complaint against his father, it is always better for him to tell it. If he thinks that his father overlooked him the other day, or half thinks that the task his father has given him is too severe, or fancies that his father is expecting too much of him, if he does not say anything at all about it, he may sulk and lose much of the loving tenderness that a child's heart should always feel. But when the child frankly says, "Father, I do not want you to think that I do not love you or that I cannot trust you, but I have a troublous thought in my mind." That is the wisest course to follow and shows a filial trust. That is the way to keep up love and confidence.

So if you hast a suspicion in your soul that mayhap your Father might put you into temptation too strong for you, tell it to Him. Tell it to Him, though it seems taking a great liberty. Though the fear may be the fruit of unbelief, yet make it known to your Lord, and do not harbor it sullenly. Remember the Lord's prayer was not made for Him, but for you, and therefore it matters from your standpoint and not from His. Our Lord's prayer is not for our Lord; it is for us, His children, and children say to their fathers ever so many things that are quite proper for them to say but that are not wise and accurate after the measure of their parents' knowledge. Their father knows what their hearts mean, and yet there may be a good deal in what they say which is foolish or mistaken.

So I look upon this prayer as exhibiting that blessed childlike confidence that tells out to its father a fear that grieves it, whether that fear be altogether correct or no. Beloved, we need not here debate the question whether God does lead into temptation or not, or whether we can fall from grace or not. It is enough that we have a fear and are permitted to tell it to our Father in heaven. Whenever you have a fear of any kind, hurry off with it to Him who loves His little ones and like a father pities them and soothes even their needless alarms.

THE TRIALS SUCH A PRAYER DEPRECATES

What are these trials that are so much feared? I do not think the prayer is intended at all to ask God to spare us from being afflicted for our good or to save us from being made to suffer as a chastisement. Of course, we should be glad to escape those things, but the prayer aims at another form of trial and may be paraphrased thus: "Save me, O Lord, from such trials and sufferings as may lead me into sin. Spare me from too great trials, lest I fall by their overcoming my patience, my faith, or my steadfastness."

Now, as briefly as I can, I will show you how men may be

led into temptation by the hand of God. The first is by the withdrawal of divine grace. Suppose for a moment—it is only a supposition—suppose the Lord were to leave us altogether; then should we perish speedily. But suppose—and this is not a barren supposition—that He were in some measure to take away His strength from us; should we not be in an evil case? Suppose He did not support our faith; what unbelief we should exhibit. Suppose He refused to support us in the time of trial so that we no longer maintained our integrity; what would become of us? Ah, the most upright man would not be upright long, nor the most holy, holy anymore.

Suppose, dear friend, His presence was withdrawn from you; what must be your portion? We are all so like to Samson in this matter that I must bring him in as the illustration, though he has often been used for that purpose by others. So long as the locks of our head are unshorn, we can do anything and everything. We can rend lions, carry gates of Gaza, and smite the armies of the foreigner. It is by the divine consecrating mark that we are strong in the power of His might, but if the Lord be once withdrawn and we attempt the work alone, then are we weak as the tiniest insect.

Another set of temptations will be found in providential conditions. The words of Agur, the son of Jakeh, shall be my illustration here:

> Remove falsehood and lies far from me;
> Give me neither poverty nor riches—
> Feed me with the food allotted to me;
> Lest I be full and deny You,

And say, "Who is the Lord?"
Or lest I be poor and steal,
And profane the name of my God. (Prov. 30:8–9)

Some of us have never known what actual want means but have from our youth up lived in social comfort. Ah, dear friends, when we see what extreme poverty has made some men do, how do we know that we should not have behaved even worse if we had been as sorely pressed as they?

And on the other hand, look at the temptations of money when men have more to spend than they can possibly need, and there is around them a society that tempts them into racing, gambling, prostitution, and all manner of iniquities. The young man who has a fortune ready to hand before he reaches years of discretion and is surrounded by flatterers and tempters all eager to plunder him—do you wonder that he is led into vice and becomes a ruined man morally? You may very well thank heaven you never knew the temptation, for if it were put in your way, you would also be in sore peril. If riches and honor allure you, follow not eagerly after them, but pray, "Lead us not into temptation."

Providential positions often try men. There is a man very much pushed for ready money in business; how shall he meet that heavy bill? If he does not meet it, there will be desolation in his family; the mercantile concern from which he now draws his living will be broken up. Everybody will be ashamed of him, his children will be outcasts, and he will be ruined. He has only to use a sum of trust money. He has no right to risk a penny of it, for it is not his, but still by its temporary use, he may perchance tide over the difficulty. The devil tells him he can put it back in a week. If he does touch that money, it will be a roguish action, but then he says, "Nobody will be hurt by it, and it will be a wonderful accommodation."

If he yields to the suggestion, and the thing goes right, there are some who would say, "Well, after all, there was not much harm in it, and it was a prudent step, for it saved him from ruin." But if it goes wrong, and he is found out, then everybody says, "It was a shameful robbery. The man ought to be transported."

But, brethren, the action was wrong in itself, and the consequences neither make it better nor worse. Do not bitterly condemn, but pray again and again, "Lead us not into temptation. Lead us not into temptation." You see, God does put men into such positions in providence at times that they are severely tried. It is for their good that they are tried, and when they can stand the trial, they magnify His grace, and they themselves become stronger. The test has beneficial uses when it can be borne, and God therefore does not always screen His children from it.

Our heavenly Father has never meant to cuddle us up and keep us out of temptation, for that is no part of the system He has wisely arranged for our education. He does not mean us to be babies in carriages all our lives. He made Adam and Eve in the garden, and He did not put an iron palisade round the tree of knowledge, and say, "You cannot get at it." No, He warned them not to touch the fruit, but they could reach the tree if they would. He meant that they should have the possibility of attaining the dignity of voluntary fidelity if they remained steadfast, but they lost it by their sin. And God means in His new creation not to shield His people from every kind of test and trial, for that were to breed hypocrites and to keep even the faithful weak and dwarfish. The Lord does sometimes put the chosen where they are tried, and we do right to pray, "Lead us not into temptation."

There are temptations arising out of physical conditions. There are some men who are moral in character because they are in health; and there are other men who are very bad, who, I do not doubt, if we knew all about them, should have some leniency shown them because of their ill health. Why, there are many people to whom to be cheerful and to be generous is no effort whatsoever, while there are others who need to labor hard to keep themselves from despair and misanthropy. Diseased livers, palpitating hearts, and injured brains are hard things to struggle against.

Does that poor old lady complain? She has only had the rheumatism thirty years, and yet she now and then murmurs! How would you be if you felt her pains for thirty minutes? I have heard of a man who complained of everybody. When he came to die, and the doctors opened his skull, they found a close-fitting brain box and that the man suffered from an irritable brain. Did not that account for a great many of his hard speeches? I do not mention these matters to excuse sin but to make you and myself treat such people as gently as we can, and pray, "Lord, do not give me such a brain box, and do not let me have such rheumatisms or such pains, because upon such a rack, I may be much worse than they are. Lead us not into temptation."

So again, mental conditions often furnish great temptations. When a man becomes depressed, he becomes tempted. Those among us who rejoice much often sink about as much as we rise, and when everything looks dark around us, Satan is sure to seize the occasion to suggest despondency. God forbid that we should excuse ourselves, but, dear brother, pray that you be not led into this temptation. Perhaps if you were as much a subject of nervousness and sinking of spirit as the friend you blame for his melancholy, you might be more blameworthy than he. Therefore pity rather than condemn.

And, on the other hand, when the spirits are exhilarated and the heart is ready to dance for joy, it is easy for levity to step in and words to be spoken amiss. Pray the Lord not to let you rise so high nor sink so low as to be led into evil. "Lead us not into temptation" must be our hourly prayer.

Further than this, there are temptations arising out of personal associations that are formed for us in the order of providence. We are bound to shun evil company, but there are cases in which, without fault on their part, persons are made to associate with bad characters. I may instance the pious child whose father is a swearer, and the godly woman lately converted whose husband remains a swearer and blasphemes the name of Christ. It is the same with workmen who have to labor in workshops, where lewd fellows at every six words let fall an oath, and pour forth that filthier language that shocks us every day more and more.

Well, if persons are obliged to work in such shops or to live in such families, there may come times when, under the lash of jest and sneer and sarcasm, the heart may be a little dismayed and the tongue may refuse to speak for Christ. Such a silence and cowardice are not to be excused, yet do not censure your brother but say, "Lord, lead me not into temptation." How know you that you would be more bold? Peter quailed before a talkative maid, and you may be cowed by a woman's tongue.

The worst temptation for a young Christian that I know of is to live with a hypocrite—a man so sanctified and demure that the young heart, deceived by appearances, fully trusts him, while the wretch is false at heart and rotten in life. And such wretches there are who, with the pretense and affectation of sanctimoniousness, will do deeds at which we might weep tears of blood. Young people are frightfully staggered, and many of them become deformed for life in their spiritual characteristics through associating with such beings as these. When you see faults caused by such common but horrible causes, say to yourself, "Lord, lead me not into temptation. I thank you for godly parents and for Christian associations and for godly examples, but what might I have been if I had been subjected to the very reverse? If evil influences had touched me when like a vessel I was upon the wheel, I might have exhibited even grosser failings than those which I now see in others."

Thus I might continue to urge you to pray, dear friends, against various temptations. But let me say, the Lord has for some men very special tests, such as may be seen in the case of Abraham. He gives him a son in his old age, and then says to him, "Take now your son, your only son Isaac, whom you love, and go to the land of Moriah, and offer him there as a burnt offering" (Gen. 22:2). You will do right to pray, "Lord, lead me not into such a temptation as that. I am not worthy to be so tried. Oh, do not so test me." I have known some Christians sit down and calculate whether they could have acted as the patriarch did. It is very foolish, dear brother. When you are called upon to do it, you will be enabled to make the same sacrifice by the grace of God, but if you are not called upon to do it, why should the power be given? Shall God's grace be left unused? Your strength shall be equal to your day, but it shall not exceed it.

Another instance is to be seen in Job. God gave Job over to Satan with a limit, and you know how Satan tormented him and tried to overwhelm him. If any man were to pray, "Lord, try me like Job," it would be a very unwise prayer. "Oh, but I could be as patient as he," say you. You are the very man who would yield to bitterness and curse your God. The man who could best exhibit the patience of Job will be the first, according to his Lord's bidding, fervently to pray, "Lead us not into temptation."

Dear friends, we are to be prepared for trial if God wills it, but we are not to court it, but are rather to pray against it, even as our Lord Jesus, though ready to drink the bitter cup, yet in an agony exclaimed, "If it is possible, let this cup pass from Me" (Matt. 26:39). Trials sought after are not such as the Lord has promised to bless. No true child asks for the rod.

To make my meaning clear, let me tell an old story. I have read in history that two men were condemned to die as martyrs in the burning days of Queen Mary. One of them boasted loudly to his companion of his confidence that he should play the man at the stake. He did not mind the suffering; he was so grounded in the gospel that he knew he should never deny it. He said that he longed for the fatal morning even as a bride for the wedding.

His companion in prison in the same chamber was a poor, trembling soul who could not and would not deny his Master, but he was very much afraid of the fire. He said he had always been sensitive of suffering, and he was in great dread that when he began to burn, the pain might cause him to deny the truth. He asked his friend to pray for him, and he spent his time weeping over his weakness and crying to God for strength. The other continually rebuked him and chided him for being so unbelieving and weak.

When they both came to the stake, he who had been so bold recanted at the sight of the fire and went back ignominiously to an apostate's life. The poor, trembling man, whose prayer had been "Lead me not into temptation," stood firm as a rock, praising and magnifying God as he was burnt to a cinder.

Weakness is our strength, and our strength is weakness. Cry unto God that He try you not beyond your strength, and in the shrinking tenderness of your conscious weakness, breathe out the prayer, "Lead us not into temptation." Then if He does lead you into the conflict, His Holy Spirit will strengthen you, and you will be brave as a lion before the adversary. Though trembling and shrinking within yourself before the throne of God, you would confront the very devil and all the hosts of hell without one touch of fear. It may seem strange, but so the case is.

LESSONS THIS PRAYER TEACHES

The first lesson from the prayer is this: Never toast your own strength. Never say, "Oh, I shall never fall into such follies and sins. They may try me, but they will find more than a match in me." Let not him who puts on his harness boast as though he were putting it off. Never indulge one thought of congratulation as to self-strength. You have no power of your own; you are as weak as water. The devil has only to touch you in the right place, and you will run according to his will. Only let a loose stone or two be moved, and you will soon see that the feeble building of your own natural virtue will come down at a run. Never court temptation by boasting your own capacity.

The next thing is, never desire trial. Dear brother, do not wish for that; you will meet with trouble soon enough. If I were a little boy at home, I do not think I should say to my brother because he had been whipped, "I am afraid I am not my father's child and fear that he does not love me because I am not smarting under the rod. I wish he would whip me just to let me know his love." No. No child would ever be so stupid. We must not for any reason desire to be afflicted or tried, but we must pray, "Lead us not into temptation."

The next thought is, never go into temptation. The man who prays, "Lead us not into temptation," and then goes into it, is a liar before God. What a hypocrite a man must be who utters this prayer and then goes off to the theatre! How false is he who offers this prayer and then stands at the bar and drinks and talks with depraved men and bedizened women! "Lead us not into temptation" is shameful profanity when it comes from the lips of men who resort to places of amusement whose moral tone is bad.

People go to church and say, "Lead us not into temptation," and then they know where temptation is to be found, and they go straight into it. You need not ask the Lord not to lead you there; He has nothing to do with you. The devil and you will go far enough without mocking God with your hypocritical prayers. The man who goes into sin willfully with his eyes open and then bends his knee and says half-a-dozen times over in his church on a Sunday morning, "Lead us not into temptation," is a hypocrite without a mask upon him. Let him take that home to himself and believe that I mean to be personal to him and to such barefaced hypocrites as he.

The last word is, if you pray God not to lead you into temptation, do not lead others there. Some seem to be singularly forgetful of the effect of their example, for they will do evil things in the presence of their children and those who look up to them. Now I pray you consider that by ill example, you destroy others as well as yourself. Do nothing, my dear brother, of which you have need to be ashamed or that you would not wish others to copy. Do the right at all times, and do not let Satan make a cat's paw of you to destroy the souls of others. Having once prayed, "Lead us not into temptation," act not the hypocrite by allowing your children to go into it.

God bless these words to us. May they sink into our souls, and if any feel that they have sinned, oh that they may now ask forgiveness through the precious blood of Christ and find it by faith in Him. When they have obtained mercy, let their next desire be that they may be kept in future from sinning as they did before, and therefore let them pray, "Lead us not into temptation." God bless you.

TITLE:
Pray Without Ceasing

TEXT:
1 Thessalonians 5:17

SUMMARY:
Spurgeon first asks what these words imply. He shows that posture, place, and time are not boundaries set in stone. He then asks what this means. He asserts there is no time when we should not pray. We should never abandon prayer and exercise it like we do our breathing. Spurgeon asks how we can apply these words. We should not let sinful interruptions keep us from praying. Spurgeon finally asks why we should obey this precept. He answers that it is a blessing and worship.

NOTABLE QUOTES

"There is no time when we may not pray."

"As perfume lies in flowers even when they do not shed their fragrance upon the gale, so let prayer lie in your hearts."

A sermon preached by Charles H. Spurgeon on March 10, 1872. *Metropolitan Tabernacle Pulpit*, vol. 18.

7

Pray Without Ceasing

Pray without ceasing.

1 THESSALONIANS 5:17

THE POSITION OF OUR TEXT is very suggestive. It comes immediately after the precept, "Rejoice always," as if that command had somewhat staggered the reader and made him ask, "How can I always rejoice?" The apostle therefore appended as answer: "Always pray." The more praying, the more rejoicing. Prayer gives a channel to the pent-up sorrows of the soul; they flow away, and in their stead, streams of sacred delight pour into the heart. When the heart is in a quiet condition and full of joy in the Lord, then also will it be sure to draw nigh unto the Lord in worship. Holy joy and prayer act and react upon each other.

Observe what immediately follows the text: "In everything give thanks." When joy and prayer are married, their firstborn child is gratitude. When we joy in God for what we have, and believingly pray to Him for more, then our souls thank Him both in the enjoyment of what we have and the prospect of what is yet to come. Those three texts are three companion pictures, representing the life of a true Christian. The central sketch is the connecting link between those on either side. These three precepts are an ornament of grace to every believer's neck. Wear them, every one of you, for glory and for beauty; rejoice always, pray without ceasing, and in everything give thanks.

WHAT DO THESE WORDS IMPLY?

Do they not imply that the use of the voice is not an essential element in prayer? It would be most unseemly even if it were possible for us to continue unceasingly to pray aloud. There would of course be no opportunity for preaching and hearing, for the exchange of friendly conversation, for business, or for any other of the duties of life. The din of so many voices would remind our neighbors rather of the worship of Baal than that of Zion.

It was never the design of the Lord Jesus that our throats, lungs, and tongues should be forever at work. Since we are to pray without ceasing, and yet could not pray with the voice without ceasing, it is clear that audible language is not essential to prayer. We may speak a thousand words that seem to be prayer and yet never pray. On the other hand, we may cry into God's ear most effectually and yet never say a word.

In the book of Exodus, God is represented as saying to

Moses, "Why do you cry to Me?" (Ex. 14:15). And yet it is not recorded that Moses had uttered so much as a single syllable at that time. It is true that the use of the voice often helps prayer. I find, personally, that I can pray best when alone if I can hear my own voice; at the same time, it is not essential, it does not enter at all into the acceptability, reality, or prevalence of prayer. Silence is as fit a garment for devotion as any that language can fashion.

It is equally clear that the posture of prayer is of no great importance, for if it were necessary that we should pray on our knees, we could not pray without ceasing, for the posture would become painful and injurious. To what end has our Creator given us feet if He desires us never to stand upon them? If He had meant us to be on our knees without ceasing, He would have fashioned the body differently and would not have endowed us with such unnecessary length of limb. It is well to pray on one's knees; it is a most fitting posture. It expresses humility, and when humility is truly felt, kneeling is a natural and beautiful token of it, but good men have also prayed flat upon their faces, sitting, standing, or in any posture, and the posture does not enter into the essence of prayer. Consent not to be placed in bondage by those to whom the bended knee is reckoned of more importance than the contrite heart.

It is clear, too, that the place is not essential to prayer, for if there were only certain holy places where prayer was acceptable, and we had to pray without ceasing, our churches ought to be extremely large, so that we might always live in them, and they would have to comprise all the arrangements necessary for human habitations. If it be true that there is some sanctity this side of a brick wall more than there is on the other side of it, if it be true that the fresh air blows away grace, and that for the highest acceptance we need groined arches, pillars, aisle, chancel, and transept, then farewell, you green lanes, fair gardens, and lovely woods, for we must, without ceasing, dwell where your fragrance and freshness can never reach us. But this is ridiculous; wherefore I gather that the frequenting of some particular place has little or nothing to do with prayer.

That precept to "pray without ceasing" at one stroke overthrows the idea of particular times wherein prayer is more acceptable or more proper than at others. If I am to pray without ceasing, then every second must be suitable for prayer, and there is not one unholy moment in the hour, nor one unaccepted hour in the day, nor one unhallowed day in the year. The Lord has not appointed a certain week for prayer, but all weeks should be weeks of prayer. Neither has He said that one hour of the day is more acceptable than another. All time is equally legitimate for supplication, equally holy, equally accepted with God, or else we should not have been told to pray without ceasing.

It is good to have your times of prayer; it is good to set apart seasons for special supplication—we have no doubt of that—but we must never allow this to gender the superstition that there is a certain holy hour for prayer in the morning, an especially acceptable hour for prayer in the evening, and a sacred time for prayer at certain seasons of the year.

Wherever we seek the Lord with true hearts, He is found of us. Whenever we cry unto him, He hears us. Every place is hallowed ground to a hallowed heart, and every day is a holy day to a holy man. From January to December, the calendar has not one date in which prayer is forbidden. All the days are red-letter days. Whether Sabbaths or weekdays, they are all accepted times for prayer.

There is one other thing implied in the text, namely, that a Christian has no right to go into any place where he could not continue to pray. Pray without ceasing? Then I am never to be in a place where I could not pray without ceasing. Hence, many worldly amusements without being particularized may be judged and condemned at once. Certain people believe in ready-made prayers, cut-and-dried for all occasions, and at the same time they believe persons to be regenerated in baptism though their lives are anything but Christian. Ought they not to provide prayers for all circumstances in which these, the dear regenerated but graceless sons and daughters of their church, are found? As, for instance, a pious collect for a young prince or nobleman who is about to go to a shooting match, that he may be forgiven for his cruelty toward those poor pigeons who are only badly wounded and made to linger in misery? As also a prayer for a religious and regenerated gentleman who is going to a horserace, and a collect for young persons upon their going to the theater to attend a very questionable play? Could not such special collects be made to order?

You revolt at the idea. Well, then, have nothing to do with that which you cannot ask God's blessing upon, have nothing to do with it, for if God cannot bless it, the devil has cursed it. Anything that is right for you to do you may consecrate with prayer, and let this be a sure gauge and test to you: if you feel that it would be an insult to the majesty of heaven to ask the Lord's blessing upon what is proposed to you, then stand clear of the unholy thing. If God does not approve, neither must you have fellowship therewith.

WHAT DO THESE WORDS MEAN?

If it does not mean we are to be always on our knees, nor always saying prayers, nor always in church or in meeting, and does not mean that we are to consider any day as unfit for praying, what then? The words mean, first, a privilege, and second, a precept.

Our Lord Jesus Christ in these words assures you that you may pray without ceasing. There is no time when we may not pray. You have here permission given to come to the mercy seat when you will, for the veil of the most holy place is rent in twain from the top to the bottom, and our access to the mercy seat is undisputed and indisputable. Kings hold their levees upon certain appointed days, and then their courtiers are admitted, but the King of kings holds a constant levee. The King of kings has called for all His people, and they may come at all times.

They were slain who went in unto the king Ahasuerus, unless he stretched out his scepter to them; but our King never withdraws His scepter, it is always stretched out, and whosoever desires to come to Him may come now and at any time. Some few of the nobility had the peculiar and special right of an audience with the Persian king at any time they chose. Now, that which was the peculiar right of a very few and of the very great is the privilege of every child of God. He may come in unto the King at all times. The dead of night is not too late for God; the breaking of the morning, when the first grey light is seen, is not too early for the Most High; at midday He is not too busy; and when the evening gathers He is not weary with His children's prayers. "Pray without ceasing" is, if I read it right, a most sweet and precious permit to the believer to pour out his heart at all times before the Lord.

The doors of the temple of divine love shall not be shut. Nothing can set a barrier between a praying soul and its God. The road of angels and of prayers is ever open. Let us but send out the dove of prayer, and we may be certain that she will return unto us with an olive branch of peace in her mouth. Evermore the Lord has regard unto the pleadings of His servants and waits to be gracious unto them.

Still, what does it mean? "Pray without ceasing" means a great truth that I cannot very well convey to you in a few words and, therefore, must try and bring out under four or five points.

Never Abandon Prayer

It means, first, never abandon prayer. Never, for any cause or reason, cease to pray. Imagine not that you must pray until you are saved and may then leave off. For those whose sins are pardoned, prayer is quite as needful as for those mourning under a sense of sin. In order that you may persevere in grace, you must persevere in prayer. Should you become experienced in grace and enriched with much spiritual knowledge, you must not dream of restraining prayer because of your gifts and graces. "Pray without ceasing," or else your flower will fade and your spiritual fruit will never ripen. Continue in prayer until the last moment of your life.

As we breathe without ceasing, so must we pray without ceasing. As there is no attainment in life, of health, or of strength, or of muscular vigor that can place a man beyond the necessity of breathing, so no condition of spiritual growth or advance in grace will allow a man to dispense with prayer.

Never give up praying, not even though Satan should suggest to you that it is in vain for you to cry unto God. If for awhile the heavens are as brass and your prayer only echoes in thunder above your head, pray on. If month after month your prayer appears to have miscarried and no reply has come to you, yet still continue to draw nigh unto the Lord. Do not abandon the mercy seat for any reason whatever. If it be a good thing that you have been asking for, and you are sure it is according to the divine will, if the vision tarry, wait for it, pray, weep, entreat, wrestle, agonize till you get that which you are praying for.

If your heart be cold in prayer, do not restrain prayer until your heart warms, but pray your soul unto heat by the help of the ever blessed Spirit who helps our infirmities. If the iron be hot, then hammer it, and if it be cold, hammer it till you heat it.

Never cease prayer for any sort of reason or argument. If the philosopher should tell you that every event is fixed, and therefore prayer cannot possibly change anything and thus must be folly, still go on with your supplications. No difficult problem concerning digestion would prevent your eating, for the result justifies the practice, and so no quibble should make us cease prayer, for the assured success of it commends it to us. You know what your God has told you, so resolve to be obedient to the divine will and "pray without ceasing." Never, never, never renounce the habit of prayer or your confidence in its power.

Never Suspend the Regular Offering of Prayer

A second meaning is this: never suspend the regular offering of prayer. You will, if you are a watchful Christian, have your times of daily devotion fixed not by superstition but for your convenience and remembrance. Be sure to keep up this daily prayer without intermission. This advice will not comprehend the whole range of the text; I am not pretending that it does. I am only mentioning it now as supplementary to other thoughts.

"Pray without ceasing," that is, never give up the morning prayer, nor the evening prayer, nor the prayer at midday if such has grown to be your habit. If you change hours and times, as you may, yet keep up the practice of regularly recurring retirement, meditation, and prayer. You may be said to continue in prayer if your habitual devotions be maintained.

I know a man who has been begging ever since I have been in London. I do not think that I ever passed the spot where he stands without seeing him there. As long as my recollection serves me, he has been begging without ceasing. Of course he has not begged when he has been asleep, and he has not begged when he has gone home to his meals, nor did you understand me to have asserted anything so absurd when I said he had begged without ceasing for years. And so, if at those times when it is proper for you to separate yourself from your ordinary labors, you continue perseveringly begging at mercy's throne, it may be with comparative correctness said of you that you pray without ceasing.

Though all hours are alike to me, I find it profitable to meet with God at set periods, for these seem to me to be like the winding up of the clock. The clock is to go all day, but there is a time for winding it up, and the little special season that we set apart and hedge round about for communion with our God seems to wind us up for the rest of the day. Therefore, if you would pray without ceasing, continue in the offering of the morning and the evening sacrifice, and let it be perpetually an ordinance with you so that your times of prayer are not broken in upon.

Labor to Be in Interjectory Prayer

That, however, is only a help, for I must add, between these times of devotion, labor to be much in interjectory prayer. While your hands are busy with the world, let your hearts still talk with God, not in twenty sentences at a time but in broken sentences and interjections. It is always wrong to present one duty to God stained with the blood of another, and that we should do if we spoiled study or labor by running away to pray at all hours. But we may, without this, let short sentences go up to heaven, and we may shoot upwards cries and single words, such as an "Ah," and "Oh," and "O that," or without words we may pray in the upward glancing of the eye or the sigh of the heart.

He who prays without ceasing uses many little darts and hand grenades of godly desire, which he casts forth at every available interval. Sometimes he will blow the furnace of his desires to a great heat in regular prayer, and at other times the sparks will continue to rise up to heaven in the form of brief words, looks, and desires.

Always Be in the Spirit of Prayer

Fourth, we must be always in the spirit of prayer. Our heart, renewed by the Holy Ghost, must be like the magnetized needle, which always has an inclination toward the pole. It does not always point to that pole. You can turn it aside if you will, but if you put your finger to that needle and force it round to the east, you have only to take away the pressure and immediately it returns to its beloved pole again. So let your heart be magnetized with prayer, so that if the finger of duty turns it away from the immediate act of prayer, there may still be the longing desire for prayer in your soul, and the moment you can do so, your heart reverts to its beloved work. As perfume lies in flowers even when they do not shed their fragrance upon the gale, so let prayer lie in your hearts.

Let All Your Actions Be Consistent with Your Prayers

Perhaps the last meaning has the most truth of the text in it: let all your actions be consistent with your prayers and be a continuation of your prayers. If I am to pray without ceasing, it cannot mean that I am always to be in the act of direct devotion, for the human mind needs variety of occupation, and it could not without producing madness or imbecility continue always in the exercise of one function. We must, therefore, change the modus or the manner of operation if we are ceaselessly to continue in prayer. We must pursue our prayers but do it in another manner.

For example, this morning I prayed to God to arouse His people to prayerfulness. Very well. As I came to this house, my soul continued to interject, "O Lord, awaken your children to prayerfulness." Now, while I am preaching to you and driving at the same point, am I not praying? Is not my sermon the continuation of my prayer, for I am desiring and aiming at the same thing? Is it not a continuing to pray when we use the best means toward the obtaining of that which we pray for? Do you not see my point? He who prays for his fellow creatures, and then seeks their good, is praying still. In this sense, there is truth in that old distich.

Loving is praying. If I seek in prayer the good of my fellow creature and then go and try to promote it, I am practically praying for his good in my actions. If I seek, as I should do, God's glory above everything, then if all my actions are meant to tend to God's glory, I am continuing to pray, though I may not be praying with my thoughts or with my lips. Oh, that our whole life might be a prayer! It can be. There can be a praying without ceasing before the Lord, though there be many pausings in what the most of men would call prayer.

Let your whole life be praying. If you change the method yet change not the pursuit, you will continue still to worship, still to adore. This I think to be the meaning of our text: never altogether abandon prayer; do not suspend the regular offering of prayer; be much in earnest interjections, be always in the spirit of prayer, and let the whole of your life be consistent with your prayer, and become a part of it.

HOW CAN WE OBEY THESE WORDS?

First, let us labor as much as we can to prevent all sinful interruptions. Then if it be impossible to be in the act of prayer always, at least let us be as much as possible in that act. Let us endeavor to keep clear, as far as we can, of anything and everything in ourselves, or round about us, that would prevent our abounding in supplication. And let us also keep clear of interruptions from the sins of others. Do others forbid us to pray? Let us not be afraid of their wrath. In private, let us always pray, and if duty calls us to do so where others observe us, let us so much fear the eye of God that we shall not dare to fear the eye of man.

Let us next avoid all unnecessary interruptions of every sort to our prayer. If we know that any matter from which we can escape tends to disturb the spirit of prayer within us, let us avoid it earnestly. Let us try, as much as possible, not to be put off the scent in prayer. Satan's object will be to distract the mind, to throw it off the rails, to divert its aim, but let us resolve before God that we will not turn aside from following hard after Him.

We sometimes allow good things to interrupt our prayer and thus make them evil. Mrs. Rowe observes in one of her letters that if the twelve apostles were preaching in the town where she lived and she could never hear them again, if it were her time for private devotion, she would not be bribed out of her closet by the hope of hearing them. I am not sure but what she might have taken another time for her private devotions and so have enjoyed both privileges, but at the same time, supposing she must have lost the prayer and have only gotten the preaching in exchange, I agree with her. It would have been exchanging gold for silver. She would be more profited in praying than she would be in hearing, for praying is the end of preaching. Preaching is but the wheat stalk, but praying is the golden grain itself, and he hath the best who gets it.

Sometimes we think we are too busy to pray. That also is a great mistake, for praying is a saving of time. You remember Luther's remark: "I have so much to do today that I shall never get through it with less than three hours' prayer." He had not been accustomed to take so much time for prayer on ordinary days, but since that was a busy day, he must needs have more communion with his God.

But perhaps our occupations begin early, and we therefore say, "How can I get alone with God in prayer?" If we have no time, we must make time, for if God has given us time for secondary duties, He must have given us time for primary ones, and to draw near to Him is a primary duty, and we must let nothing set it on one side. There is no real need to sacrifice any duty; we have time enough for all if we are not idle, and, indeed, the one will help the other instead of clashing with it. God can multiply our ability to make use of time. If we give the Lord His due, we shall have enough for all necessary purposes. In this matter, seek first the kingdom of God and His righteousness, and all these things shall be added to you. Your other engagements will run smoothly if you do not forget your engagement with God.

We must, dear friends, in order to pray without ceasing, strive against indolence in prayer. I believe that no man loves prayer until the Holy Spirit has taught him the sweetness and value of it. If you have ever prayed without ceasing, you will pray without ceasing. The men who do not love to pray must be strangers to its secret joy. When prayer is a mechanical act and there is no soul in it, it is a slavery and a weariness. But when it is really living prayer, and when the man prays because he is a Christian and cannot help praying, when he prays along the street, in his business, in the house, in the field—when his whole soul is full of prayer—then he cannot have too much of it. He will not be backward in prayer who meets Jesus in it, but he who knows not the well-beloved will count it a drudgery.

Let us avoid, above all things, lethargy and indifference in prayer. Oh, it is a dreadful thing that ever we should insult the majesty of heaven by words from which our heart has gone. I must, my spirit, I must school you to this, that you must have communion with God, and if in your prayer you do not talk with God, keep on praying till you do. Come not away from the mercy seat till you have prayed.

Beloved brother, say unto your soul thus: "Here have I come to the throne of grace to worship God and seek His blessing, and I am not going away till I have done this. I will not rise from my knees because I have spent my customary minutes, but here will I pray till I find the blessing." Satan will often leave off tempting when he finds you thus resolute in prayer. Brethren, we need waking up. Routine grows upon us. We get into the mill-horse way—round and round and round the mill. From this may God save us. It is deadly. A man may pray twenty years with regularity, as far as the time goes and the form goes, and never have prayed a single grain of prayer in the whole period. One real groan fetched from the heart is worth a million litanies, one living breath from a gracious soul is worth ten thousand collects. May we be kept awake by God's grace, praying without ceasing.

And we must take care, again, if we would perform this duty, that we fight against anything like despair of being heard. If we have not been heard after six times, we must, as Elijah, go again seven times. If our Peter is in prison and the church has prayed God to liberate him, and he still is in fetters bound in the inner prison, let us pray on, for one of these days, Peter will knock at the gate. Be importunate; heaven's gate does not open to every runaway knock. Knock and knock and knock again, and add to your knocking and to your asking seeking, and be not satisfied till you get a real answer.

Never cease from prayer through presumption; guard against that. Feel, O Christian, that you always need to pray. Say not, "I am rich and increased in goods, and have need of nothing." You are by nature still naked and poor and miserable; therefore, persevere in prayer, and buy of the Lord fine gold and clean raiment, that you may be rich and fitly clothed.

WHY OBEY THESE WORDS?

Of course, we should obey it because it is of divine authority, but, moreover, we should attend to it because the Lord always deserves to be worshiped, and prayer is a method of worship. Continue, therefore, always to render to your Creator, your Preserver, your Redeemer, your Father, the homage of your prayers. With such a King, let us not be slack in homage. Let us pay Him the revenue of praise continually. Evermore may we magnify and bless His name. His enemies curse Him; let us bless Him without ceasing.

Moreover, brethren, the spirit of love within us surely prompts us to draw near to God without ceasing. Christ is our husband. Is the bride true to her marriage vows if she cares not for her beloved's company? God is our Father. What sort of a child does not desire to climb its father's knee and receive a smile from its father's face? If you and I can live day after day and week after week without anything like communion with God, how does the love of God dwell in us? "Pray without ceasing" because the Lord never ceases to love you, never ceases to bless you, and never ceases to regard you as His child.

"Pray without ceasing," for you want a blessing on all the work you are doing. Is it common work? "Unless the LORD builds the house, they labor in vain who build it" (Ps. 127:1). Is it business? "It is vain for you to rise up early, to sit up late, to eat the bread of sorrows" (Ps. 127:2), for without God you cannot prosper. You are taught to say, "Give us this day our daily bread"—an inspired prayer for secular things. Oh, consecrate your seculars by prayer. And if you are engaged in God's service, what work is there in which you can hope for success without His blessing? To teach the young, to preach the gospel, to distribute tracts, to instruct the ignorant, do not all these want His blessing? What are they if that favor be denied? Pray, therefore, as long as you work.

You are always in danger of being tempted; there is no position in life in which you may not be assaulted by the enemy. "Pray without ceasing," therefore. A man who is going along a dark road where he knows that there are enemies, if he must be alone and has a sword with him, he carries it drawn in his hand to let the robbers know that he is ready for them. So Christian, "pray without ceasing;" carry your sword in your hand; wave that mighty weapon of all prayer of which Bunyan speaks. Never sheath it; it will cut through coats of mail. You need fear no foe if you can but pray. As you are tempted without ceasing, so "pray without ceasing."

You need always to pray, for you always want something. In no condition are you so rich as not to need something from your God. It is not possible for you to say, "I have all things," or, if you can, you have them only in Christ, and from Christ, you must continue to seek them. As you are always in need, so beg always at mercy's gate. Moreover, blessings are always waiting for you. Angels are ready with favors that you know not of, and you have but to ask and have. Oh, could you see what might be had for the asking you would not be so slack. The priceless benisons of heaven that lie on one side as yet, oh, did you but perceive that they are only waiting for you to pray, you would not hesitate a moment. The man who knows that his farming is profitable, and that his land brings forth abundantly, will be glad to sow a broader stretch of land another year, and he who knows that God answers prayer and is ready still to answer it, that man will open his mouth yet wider that God may fill it.

Continue to pray, brethren, for even if you should not want prayer yourself, there are others who do—the dying, the sick, the poor, the ignorant, the backsliding, the blaspheming, the heathen at home, and the heathen abroad. "Pray without ceasing," for the enemy works incessantly, and as yet the kingdom has not come unto Zion. You shall never be able to say, "I left off praying, for I had nothing to pray for." This side of heaven, objects for prayer are as multitudinous as the stars of the sky.

Suppose, dear brethren, there were no conversions in our midst; would not you pray? And since there are a great many conversions, should that be a reason for leaving off? Shall we worship God the less because He gives us more? Instead of one prayer that would go up were there no conversions, there should be ten now that He continues to work salvation among us.

Suppose we were divided and had many schisms and jealousies and bickerings; would not the faithful ones pray in bitterness of spirit? Will you not pray since there are no divisions and much Christian love? Surely, I say again, you will not treat God the worse because He treats you the better. That were foolish indeed.

Suppose we were surrounded today with hosts of persecutors and that error everywhere crept into our midst and did us damage, would you not pray, you who love the Lord? And now that we live in days of peace—and error, though it prowls around, is kept out of our fold—will you not commune with the Lord all the more? I will say yet again: shall we pray the less because God gives the more? Oh no, but the better He is to us, the more let us adore and magnify His name.

TITLE:
Thanksgiving and Prayer

TEXT:
Psalm 65:11

SUMMARY:
Spurgeon first highlights crowning mercies, suggesting special and crowning thanksgiving. We pray with inward motivations of gratitude. The second point Spurgeon makes is that paths to abundance should be ways of duty. He exhibits how the people of God are happy that rely on His goodness and grace. If we are faint, we find strength in turning to God.

NOTABLE QUOTES
"Happy, happy are the people who worship such a God, whose coming is ever a coming of goodness and of grace to His creatures."

"Close access to God in wrestling prayer is sure to make the believer strong—if not happy."

A sermon preached by Charles H. Spurgeon on September 27, 1863. *Metropolitan Tabernacle Pulpit*, vol. 9.

8

Thanksgiving and Prayer

*You crown the year with Your goodness,
And Your paths drip with abundance.*

PSALM 65:11

POSSIBLY OBJECTIONS MIGHT have been raised to a day of thanksgiving for the abundant harvest if it had been ordered or suggested by the government. Certain brethren are so exceedingly tender in their consciences upon the point of connection between church and state that they would have thought it almost a reason for not being thankful at all if the government had recommended them to celebrate a day of public thanksgiving. Although I have no love to the unscriptural union of church and state, I should, on this occasion, have hailed an official request for a national recognition of the special goodness of God.

However, none of us can feel any abjection arising in our

minds if it be now agreed that today we will praise our ever-bounteous Lord and, as an assembly, record our gratitude to the God of the harvest. We are probably the largest assembly of Christian people in the world, and it is well that we should set the example to the smaller churches. Doubtless many other believers will follow in our track, and so a public thanksgiving will become general throughout the country. I hope to see every congregation in the land raising a special offering unto the Lord, to be devoted either to His church, to the poor, to missions, or some other holy end. Yes, I would have every Christian offer willingly unto the Lord as a token of his gratitude to the God of providence.

Without any preface, we will divide our text as it divides itself. Here we have crowning mercies calling for crowning gratitude. And in the same verse, paths of abundance, which should be to us ways of delight. When we have talked upon these two points, we may meditate for a few moments upon the whole subject and endeavor, as God shall help us, to see what duties it suggests.

CROWNING MERCIES SUGGEST SPECIAL AND CROWNING THANKSGIVING

All the year round, every hour of every day, God is richly blessing us. Both when we sleep and when we wake, His mercy waits upon us. The sun may leave off shining, but our God will never cease to cheer His children with His love. Like a river, His lovingkindness is always flowing with a fullness inexhaustible as

His own nature, which is its source. Like the atmosphere that always surrounds the earth and is always ready to support the life of man, the benevolence of God surrounds all His creatures. In it, as in their element, they live and move and have their being.

Yet as the sun on summer days appears to gladden us with beams more warm and bright than at other times, and as rivers are at certain seasons swollen with the rain, and as the atmosphere itself on occasions is fraught with more fresh, more bracing, or more balmy influences than heretofore, so is it with the mercy of God. It has its golden hours, its days of overflow when the Lord magnifies His grace and lifts high His love before the sons of men.

If we begin with the blessings of the nether springs, we must not forget that, for the race of man, the joyous days of harvest are a special season of excessive favor. It is the glory of autumn that the ripe gifts of providence are then abundantly bestowed; it is the mellow season of realization, whereas all before was but hope and expectation. Great is the joy of harvest. Happy are the reapers who fill their arms with the liberality of heaven. The psalmist tells us that the harvest is the crowning of the year.

What if I compare the opening spring to the proclamation of a new prince, the latest born of Father Time? With the musical voices of birds and the joyful lowing of herds, a new era of fertility is ushered in. Every verdant meadow and every leaping brook hears the joyful proclamation and feels a new life within. The little hills rejoice on every side; they shout for joy and sing.

Throughout the warm months of summer, the royal year is robing itself in beauty and adorning itself in sumptuous array. What with the plates of ivory yielded by the lilies, the rubies of the rose, the emeralds of the meads, and all manner of fair colors from the many flowers, we may well say that "Solomon in all his glory was not arrayed like one of these" (Matt. 6:29). No studs of silver or rows of jewels can vie with the ornaments of the year. No garments of needlework of divers colors can match the glorious vesture of time's reigning Son.

But the moment of the coronation, when earth feels most the sway of the year, is in the fullness of autumn. Then when the fields are covered with a cloth of gold, and fruits are glowing with the rich hues of ripeness, and the leaves are burnished with inimitable perfection of tint and shade, then with a coronal of divine goodness amidst the glad shouts of toiling swains and the songs of rejoicing maidens, the year is crowned. Upon a throne of golden corn, with the peaceful sickle for His scepter, sits the crowned year bearing the goodness of the Lord as a coronet upon His placid brow.

Or what if we compare the year to a conqueror, striving at first with stern winter, wrestling hard against all his boisterous attacks, at last joyfully conquering in the fair days of spring, riding in triumph throughout the summer along a pathway strewed with flowers, and at last mounting the throne, amidst the festivities of harvest, while the Lord in lovingkindness puts a diadem of beauty and goodness upon its head?

We may forget the harvest, living as we do so far from rural labors, but those who must watch the corn as it springs up and track it through all its numberless dangers until the blade becomes the full corn in the ear cannot, surely, forget the wonderful goodness and mercy of God when they see the harvest safely stored.

My brethren, if we require any considerations to excite us to gratitude, let us think for a moment of the effect upon our country of a total failure of the crops. Suppose today it were reported that as yet the corn was not carried, that the continued showers had made it sprout and grow till there was no hope of its being of any further use and that it might as well be left in the fields. What dismay would that message carry into every cottage! Who among us could contemplate the future without dismay? All faces would gather blackness. All classes would sorrow, and even the throne itself might fitly be covered with sackcloth at the news.

My brethren, should we not rejoice that this is not our case and that our happy land rejoices in plenty? If the plant had utterly failed and the seed had rotted under the clods, we should have been quick enough to murmur; how is it that we are so slow to praise? Take a lower view of the matter, suppose even a partial scarcity. At this juncture, when one arm of our industry is paralyzed, how serious would have been this calamity! With a staple commodity withdrawn from us, with the daily peril of war at our gates, it would have been a fearful trial to have suffered scarcity of bread.

Shall we not bless and praise our covenant God who permits not the appointed weeks of harvest to fail? Sing together, all ye to whom bread is the staff of life, and rejoice before Him who loadeth you with benefits. We have none of us any adequate idea of the amount of happiness conferred upon a nation by a luxuriant crop. Every man in the land is the richer for it. To the poor man, the difference is of the utmost importance. His three shillings are now worth four; there is more bread for the children or more money for clothes. Millions are benefited by God's once opening His liberal hand.

When the Hebrews went through the desert, there were but some two or three million of them, and yet they sang sweetly of Him who fed His chosen people. In our own land alone, we have ten times the number; have we no hallowed music for the God of the whole earth? Reflect upon the amazing population of our enormous city—consider the immense amount of poverty—think how greatly at one stroke that poverty has been relieved! A generous contribution would be but as the drop of a bucket to the relief afforded by a fall in the price of bread.

Let us not despise the bounty of God because this great boon comes in a natural way. If every morning when we awoke we saw fresh loaves of bread put into our cupboard, or the morning's meal set out upon the table, we should think it a miracle, but if our God blesses our own exertions and prospers our own toil to the same end, is it not equally as much a ground for praising and blessing His name? I would I had this morning the tongue of the eloquent, or even my own usual strength, to excite you to gratitude by the spectacle of the multitudes of beings whom God has made happy by the fruit of the field.

But how shall we give crowning thanksgiving for this crowning mercy of the year? We can do it, dear friends, by the inward emotions of gratitude. Let our hearts be warmed. Let our spirits remember, meditate, and think upon this goodness of the Lord. Meditation upon this mercy may tend to nourish in you the tenderest feelings of affection, and your souls will be knit to the Father of spirits, who pities His children.

Again, praise Him with your lips; let psalms and hymns employ your tongues today, and tomorrow when we meet together at the prayer meeting, let us turn it rather into a praise meeting, and let us laud and magnify His name from whose bounty all this goodness flows.

But I think, also, we should thank Him by our gifts. The Jews of old never tasted the fruit either of the barley or of the wheat harvest till they had sanctified it to the Lord by the Feast of Ingatherings. There was, early in the season, the barley harvest. One sheaf of this barley was taken and waved before the Lord with special sacrifices, and then afterwards, the people feasted. Fifty days afterwards came the wheat harvest, when two loaves made of the new flour were offered before the Lord in sacrifice, together with burnt offerings, peace offerings, meat offerings, drink offerings, and abundant sacrifices of thanksgivings to show that the people's thankfulness was not stinted.

No man ate either of the ears, or grain, or corn ground and made into bread until first of all he had sanctified his substance by the dedication of somewhat unto the Lord. And shall we do less than the Jew? Shall he, for types and shadows, express his gratitude in a solid manner, and shall not we? Did he offer unto the Lord, whom he scarce knew, and bow before that Most High God who hid His face amidst the smoke of burning rams and bullocks? And shall not we who see the glory of the Lord in the face of Christ Jesus come unto Him and bring to Him our offerings? The Old Testament ordinance was, you "shall not appear before the LORD empty-handed" (Deut. 16:16), and let that be the ordinance of today. Let us come into His presence, each man bearing His offering of thanksgiving unto the Lord.

Furthermore, beloved, we have heard of heavenly harvests, the outflowing of the upper springs, which in days of yore awakened the church of God to loudest praise. There was the harvest of Pentecost. Christ, having been sown in the ground like a grain of wheat, sprang up from it, and in His resurrection and ascension was like the waved sheaf before the Lord. Let us never forget that resurrection that crowned the year of God's redeemed with goodness. It was a terrible year indeed; it began in the howling tempests of Christ's poverty and want and shame and suffering and death. It seemed to have no spring and no summer, yet it was crowned with an abundant harvest when Jesus Christ rose from the dead.

Fifty days after the resurrection came the Pentecost. The barley harvest had been passed wherein the wave sheaf was offered, then came the days of wheat harvest. Peter and the eleven with him became the reapers, and three thousand souls fell beneath the gospel sickle. There was great joy in the city of Jerusalem that day—nay, all the saints who heard thereof were glad, and heaven itself, catching the divine enthusiasm, rang with harvest joy. It is recorded that the saints ate their bread with gladness and singleness of heart, praising God. Pentecost was a crowning mercy, and it was remembered by the saints with crowning thanks.

Here it is, O well beloved flock of my care and love, that I ask your gratitude, mainly and chiefly. My brethren, how the Lord has cheered and comforted our hearts while He has crowned our years with His goodness. Here these ten years have I, as He has enabled me, preached the gospel among you. We have seen no excitement, no stirrings of an unwarranted fanaticism, no wildfires have been kindled, and yet see how the multitude have listened to the gospel with unceasing attention. The surging crowds at yonder doors prove that, as in the days of John the Baptist, so it is now, the kingdom of heaven suffers violence, and every man presses into it.

As for conversions, has not the Lord been pleased to give them to us as constantly as the sun rises in His place? Scarce a sermon without the benediction of the Most High—many of them preached in weakness, which none of you have known but the speaker, preached at times with throbs of heart and pantings of anguish, which have made the preacher go home mourning that he ever preached at all. And yet success has come, and souls have been saved, and the preacher's heart has been made to sing for joy, for the seed rots not, the furrows are good, the field has been well prepared, and where the seed falls, it brings forth a hundredfold to the praise and honor of the Most High.

Brethren, we must not forget this. We might have preached for naught; we might have ploughed the thankless rock and gathered no sheaves. Why then does He bless us? Is it our worthiness? Ah, no. Is it for ought in the preacher or in the hearers? God forbid that we should think such a thing. It has been the sovereign mercy of God that has prospered His own truth among us, and shall we not for this praise and bless His name?

If we, as a church, do not continue to be as prayerful and as earnest as we have been, the Lord may justly make us like Shiloh, which He deserted, until it became a desolation. Nay,

I venture to say, if we do not progress in earnestness, if you, my hearers, do not become more than ever devoted to the Lord's cause, if there be not more and more of an earnest missionary spirit stirred up and nurtured among us, we may expect the Lord to turn away from us and find another people who shall more worthily repay His favors.

Who knows but you may have come to the kingdom for such a time as this? Perhaps the Lord intends, by some of you, to save multitudes of souls, to stir up His churches, and to awaken the slumbering spirit of religion. Will you prove unworthy? Will you say, "I pray you have me excused." Will you not rather, in looking back upon the plentiful harvest of souls reaped in this place, consider that you are in debt to God and therefore give to Him the fullest consecration that believers can offer because of the crowning mercies which we as a Church receive?

Beloved, we are looking forward to a time when this world's year shall be crowned with God's goodness in the highest and most boundless sense. Centuries are flying, and yet the darkness lingers. Time grows old, and yet the idols sit upon their thrones. Christ reigns not yet; His unsuffering kingdom has not come; the scepters are still in the hands of despots, and slaves still fret in iron bonds. In vain, in vain, O earth, have you expected brighter days, for still the thick and heavy night rests over your sons.

But the day shall come—and the signs of its coming are increasing in their brightness—the day shall come when the harvest of the world shall be reaped. Christ has not died in vain; He redeemed the world with His blood, and the whole world He will have. From eastern coast to western, Christ must reign. Yet will the seed of the woman chase the powers of darkness back to their evil habitation. Yet shall He pierce the crooked serpent and cut leviathan in the depths of the sea. Yet shall the trumpet ring, and the multitudes represented in Him when He rose as the great wave sheaf shall rise from the dead from land and sea. And yet, in the day of His appearing, shall the kings of the earth yield up their sovereignty, and all nations shall call Him blessed.

Tarry awhile, beloved, wait yet a little season, and when you shall hear the shout, "Alleluia! For the Lord God Omnipotent reigns!" (Rev. 19:6), then shall you know that He crowns the year with His goodness.

PATHS OF ABUNDANCE SHOULD BE WAYS OF DUTY

When the conqueror journeys through the nations, his paths drop blood; fire and vapor of smoke are in his track, and tears, groans, and sighs attend him. But where the Lord journeys, His "paths drip with abundance."

When the kings of old made a progress through their dominions, they caused a famine wherever they tarried, for the greedy courtiers who swarmed in their camp devoured all things like locusts and were as greedily ravenous as palmer worms and caterpillars. But where the great King of kings journeys, He enriches the land; His "paths drip with abundance." By a bold Hebrew metaphor—and the Hebrew poetry certainly seems to be the most sublime in its conceptions—the clouds are represented as the chariots of God: He "makes the clouds His chariot" (Ps. 104:3). And as the Lord rides upon the heavens in the greatness of His strength, and in His excellency on the sky, the rains drop down upon the lands, and so the wheel tracks of the Lord are marked by the abundance that makes glad the earth. Happy, happy are the people who worship such a God, whose coming is ever a coming of goodness and of grace to His creatures.

We see, then, dear friends, that in providence, wherever the Lord comes, His "paths drip with abundance." He may sometimes seem to pinch His people and bring them into want, but if there be not an abundance of outward good, there will be an abundance of inward mercy. Even the trials that the Lord scatters like coals of fire in His path do but burn up the weeds and warm the heart of the soil. Do but trust the Lord and appeal to Him in all your straits and difficulties, and you shall find that when He comes forth out of His hiding place for your help, His paths shall drip abundance; your poverty shall be removed, and your dejection of spirit shall be cheered.

Beloved, we believe that our text has a fullness of meaning if it be viewed in a spiritual sense: "His paths drip with abundance." In the use of the means, the sinner will find God's paths drip with abundance. Are you hungry and thirsty? Does your soul faint within you? Are you longing to be satisfied with favor? Then, sinner, wait upon the Lord, and hearken diligently unto the message of His gospel; be constantly searching the Scriptures or listening to His truth as it is proclaimed in thine ears.

The Person of Christ

Especially, sinner, remember that the ways of the Lord are to be seen in the person of Christ. Go to those hands that are the trackways of divine justice; go to those feet that are the pathways of infinite love; explore that side where deep affection dwells, and you shall find abundance of mercy dropping there. No sinner ever did come to God and was sent empty away. You may attend the means, I grant you, and yet find no comfort, for means are not always God's paths. But you cannot come to Christ—you cannot rest in Him—and be disappointed. Trust in Him at all times, and however deep your poverty, it shall have a superabundant supply.

You also who are His people, I know that sometimes your souls grow faint. Weary with the wilderness, worn with its cares, torn with its briars, you come up to the house of God, and if you come there to see your Master—and not merely to join in the routine of service—if you come there seeking after Him and panting for Him as the hart pants for the water brooks, you will find that the commonest services—poor though be the minister and plain the place and simple the people, though the music may have but little charm for the ear of taste and the words of the speaker may have none of the trappings of oratory—yet sweet to you shall be the worship of God's house, and you shall find that "his paths drip with abundance."

The Ordinances

So, too, in the use of those precious ordinances—baptism and the Lord's Supper. You who know the truth, and are made free by it, shall find that those paths drip with abundance. I believe many of you are lean and starved because you are not obedient to your Lord's command in baptism. You know what He bids you do, but you stand back from it. You comprehend your duty, and perhaps you say you are Baptists in principle, forgetting that this very principle of yours will condemn you unless you carry it out. In keeping that commandment there is a great reward.

It is peculiarly so at the Lord's Table. I would not give up the Lord's Supper as a means of grace for ought that could be devised. To the godless, it must ever be a condemnation, but to the saint of God who comes there desiring to be fed with the flesh of Christ, it becomes a feast indeed. I do trust, dear friends, that in a very short time, we shall celebrate the Lord's Supper every Sabbath day. I am convinced that a weekly celebration is scriptural, and I see more and more the need of it. I think it is an ordinance to which we ought not to prescribe our own times and our own seasons where the Word of God is so very express and so plain. Such was apostolic custom. Indeed, if there were no apostolic precedent, methinks the sweetness of the service and the delightful nature of the ordinance might suggest to Christians that it was well to have it frequently. We cannot be satisfied once a month with communion with Christ, and methinks we hardly ought to be satisfied with the sign itself so seldom.

Prayer

Beloved, the Lord has other paths besides those of the open means of grace, and these too drip abundance. Especially let me mention the path of prayer. No believer ever says, "My leanness, my leanness; woe unto me" who is much in the closet. Starving souls generally live at a distance from the mercy seat. Close access to God in wrestling prayer is sure to make the believer strong—if not happy. The nearest place to the gate of heaven is the throne of the heavenly grace. Much alone, and you will have much assurance; little alone with God, your religion will be very shallow. You shall have many doubts and fears and but little of the joy of the Lord.

Let us see to it, beloved, that since the soul-enriching path of prayer is open to the very weakest saint, since no high attainments are required, since you are not bidden to come because you are an advanced saint but freely invited if you be a saint at all, let us see to it that we be often in the way of private devotion. Be much on your knees, for so Elijah drew the rain upon famished Israel's fields.

Communion with Christ

The like, certainly, I may say of the secret path of communion. Oh! The delights which are to be had by that man who has fellowship with Christ! Earth hath no words that can set forth the holy mirth of the soul that leans on Jesus's bosom. Few Christians understand it; they live in the lowlands and seldom climb to the top of Nebo. They live outside; they come not into the holy place; they take not up the privilege of priesthood. At a distance they see the sacrifice, but they sit not down with the priest to eat thereof and to enjoy the fat of the burnt offering. Brother, sister, sit ever under the shadow of

Jesus; come up to that palm tree and take hold of the branches thereof; let your beloved be unto you as the apple tree among the trees of the wood, and you shall find a never-failing fruit, which shall ever be sweet unto your taste.

Faith

I must not forget that the path of faith, too, is a path that drips with abundance. It is a strange path—few walk in it, even of professors; but they who in temporals and in spirituals have learned to lean on God alone shall find it a path of abundance. Wait only upon God; let your expectation be from Him. The young lions may lack and suffer hunger, but you shall not want any good thing, for the paths of the Lord shall drip with abundance to you.

THE HOLY SPIRIT

O my dear hearers, I would to God the Lord would come into the midst of our churches and congregations by His Spirit, then would His path drip with abundance. We have a multitude of complaints at different times of the dullness and lethargy of the churches, but what we need is more of the presence of the Holy Spirit—more of the holy baptism of His sacred influences. However experienced we may be in sacred service, you and I cannot serve God effectually, nor see any power resting on our ministry, except as we get more of the Spirit of the living God.

I would that the churches laid to heart more and more the real need of the times. We have been building hosts of chapels lately and raising thousands of pounds, and because there were revivals, we have been thinking that we are in a good state. Now, I venture to say that all our denominations are in a bad state. Why, our places of worship do not operate as they should upon the people. They are, in most places, mere clubs where good people spend their Sundays, but the outlying mass is not touched. We have lost the old fire to a great extent, the divine enthusiasm, the Pentecostal furor. That sacred flame of the first apostles, which is so much needed if ever we are to startle a dying world, is almost extinct.

And in this place, where God has favored us with much of His presence, we are getting into very much the same condition. How many of you who once were earnest now are as cold as slabs of ice! Some of you do hardly anything for my Lord and Master. Converted, I trust you are, but where is your first love? Where is the love of your espousals that made some of you talk of Jesus by day and dream of Him by night?

O for a return to God's paths—O for a revival once again in the midst of the churches. Ten years ago, we could speak honestly that the churches were almost dead, but I think they are worse now because they have cherished the idea that they are not so dead as they were. We are as bad as ever, with a name to live, whereas we are dead. Oh that some trumpet voice could wake our sleeping churches once again.

Can ye live without souls saved? If you can, I cannot. Can you live without London being enlightened with the light of God? If you can so live, I pray my Master let me die. Can you bear to fight and win no victories? To sow and reap no harvests?

Brethren, if you are right, you cannot endure it, but you must endure it till the Lord comes forth. Let us pray therefore with might and main, with a holy violence that will take no denial; let us pray the Lord to come forth out of His hiding place, for His "paths drip with abundance," and there is abundance to be found nowhere else besides.

PRACTICAL APPLICATIONS

And now I close. The whole subject seems to give us one or two suggestions as to matters of duty. "You crown the year with Your goodness." One suggestion is this: some of you in this house are strangers to God. You have been living as His enemies, and you will probably die so. But what a blessing it would be if a part of the crown of this year should be your conversion! "The harvest is past, the summer is ended, and we are not saved" (Jer. 8:20 KJV). But oh, what a joy, if this very day you should turn unto God and live! Remember, the way of salvation was freely proclaimed last Sabbath morning; it runs in this style: "This is the work of God, that you believe in Him whom He sent" (John 6:29). Soul, if this day you trust in Christ, it shall be your spiritual birthday; it shall be unto you the beginning of days: emancipated from your chains, delivered from the darkness of the valley of the shadow of death, you shall be the Lord's free man. What say you? Oh that the Spirit of God would bring you this day to turn unto Him with full purpose of heart.

Another suggestion. Would not the Lord crown this year with His goodness if He would move some of you to do more for Him than you have ever done before? Cannot you think of some new thing that you have forgotten but that is in the power of your hand? Can you not do it for Christ today? Some fresh soul you have never conversed with, some fresh means of usefulness you have never attempted?

And last, would not it be well for us if the Lord would crown this year with His goodness by making us begin from this day to be more prayerful? Let our prayer meetings have more at them, and let everyone in his closet pray more for the preacher, pray more for the church. Let us, every one of us, give our hearts anew to Christ. What say you today, to renew your consecration vow? Let us say to Him, "Here, Lord, I give myself away to you once more. You have bought me with your blood; accept me over again. From this good hour, I will begin a new life for a second time if your Spirit be with me. Help me, Lord, for Jesus Christ's sake." Amen.

Acknowledgments

AS WITH ANY WRITING PROJECT, this book would not have come to completion without the sacrifice and support of many. I remain profoundly indebted to each one of them.

At the personal level, my life and ministry are enabled and enriched by the prayers and encouragement of my family. God has given me a wife, Karen, and children, Anne-Marie, Caroline, William, Alden, and Elizabeth, who bless me beyond measure. I love each one of you unconditionally and beyond measure.

At the institutional level, my colleagues and office staff likewise are an invaluable source of support and encouragement. Most especially, I'm thankful for Tyler Sykora, Dawn Philbrick, Lauren Hanssen, Wesley Rule, and Justin Love. I'm also thankful for Russ Meek, who provided keen editorial assistance. Each one of these men and women is an absolute delight to serve with, and they each go about their daily tasks with graciousness and competence. Thank you.

I'm thankful to the team at Moody Publishers, most especially Drew Dyck and Kevin Mungons. Thank you for believing in this project and for working with me to bring it to completion.

Last, and most of all, I'm indebted to my Lord and Savior, Jesus Christ. Like every other ministerial undertaking, none of this would be possible without His grace, calling, and enabling. May this book, and all that I do, bring Him much glory.

When Spurgeon speaks, you'd be wise to listen.

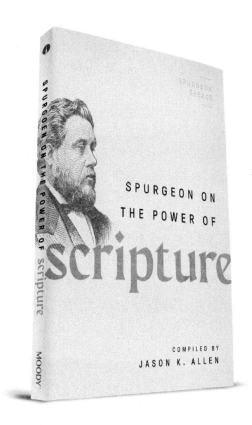

MOODY Publishers®

From the Word to Life®

Volume 2 of the Spurgeon Speaks series focuses on the power of God's Word. Spurgeon's love for the Bible will encourage you too. Presented in lovely editions that you'll be proud to own, the series offers readings on topics of importance to the Prince of Preachers.

978-0-8024-2629-1 | also available as an eBook

DISCOVER WHY THE FUNDAMENTALS OF THE REFORMATION STILL MATTER TODAY

MOODY Publishers

From the Word to Life

Sola is a winsome, inspiring introduction to the five pillars of the Reformation, showing not just what they are but why they're important for the Christian life today. Edited and compiled by Jason Allen, *Sola* will illuminate these core truths—and it may just get you excited about nerdy Latin phrases, as well!

978-0-8024-1873-9 | also available as an eBook

Collected insights from A.W. Tozer on common topics for the Christian life

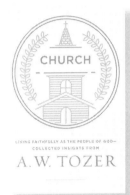

978-0-8024-1828-9

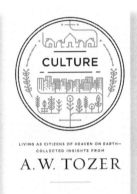

978-1-60066-801-2

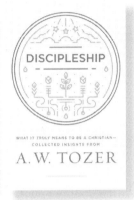

978-1-60066-804-3

978-0-8024-1520-2

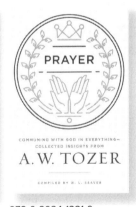

978-0-8024-1381-9

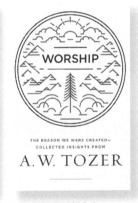

978-0-8024-1603-2

also available as eBooks

From the Word to Life

"Only God can justify the ungodly, but He can do it to perfection. He casts our sins behind His back; He blots them out. He says that though they be sought for, they shall not be found."
—C. H. SPURGEON

MOODY Publishers

From the Word to Life

In an age of limited travel and isolated nations, C. H. Spurgeon preached to over 10,000,000 people in person—sometimes up to ten times per week. It is in this classic work that Spurgeon most clearly presents the message of salvation—man's ultimate need and God's unique provision—both simply and sincerely, for honest seekers and zealous witnesses alike.

978-0-8024-5452-2 | also available as an eBook